Islam and Education
the manipulation and misrepresentation
of a religion

Islam and Education
the manipulation and misrepresentation of a religion

Lynn Revell

Trentham Books
Stoke on Trent, UK and Sterling, USA

Trentham Books Limited
Westview House   22883 Quicksilver Drive
734 London Road   Sterling
Oakhill   VA 20166-2012
Stoke on Trent   USA
Staffordshire
England ST4 5NP

First published 2012

British Library Cataloguing-in-Publication Data
A catalogue record for this book is available from the
British Library

ISBN 978-1-85856-489-0

Cover picture: Ran Revell [aged 10]

Designed and typeset by Trentham Books Ltd, Chester
Printed and bound in Great Britain by 4edge Limited, Hockley

Contents

Acknowledgements • vi

Introductions • vii

Chapter 1
Islam and World Religions • 1

Chapter 2
The limits of multiculturalism • 21

Chapter 3
Teaching and learning – the raw materials • 37

Chapter 4
Islam, education and the Home Office • 65

Chapter 5
Tolerance and Representation • 97

Books Discussed • 119

References • 123

Index • 133

For Angus Pryor

Acknowledgments

I would like to thank Canterbury Christ Church University for granting the generous time for the writing of this book and especially for providing so many of the textbooks for review in chapter three. I am grateful to friends and colleagues who generated a stimulating environment at work and particularly Hazel Bryan who gave enormous encouragement and read the final proofs. My thanks to my daughter Ran for drawing the beautiful picture on the cover of the book.

Students and teachers who shared their experiences of talking to children about Islam and equality have had a significant effect on the shape of this book and their research was often challenging and inspirational. I owe thanks to Jenny Fogarty for her collaboration in research on children and Islam that underpinned this book. I am in debt to Farid Panjwani because it was his work on the representation of Islam in the agreed syllabi that raised questions about my own work and responsibilities in the education of teachers. I would also like to thank Joyce Miller for her generous interview and her insights into the development of *RE*silience. My last thanks are to Gillian Klein and her commitment to this book.

Introduction

This book challenges the core assumptions about equality and power which inform the way Islam is represented in education in Britain. Many dominant approaches and resources used to teach Islam are motivated by a desire to present Islam fairly and sympathetically, but because most ignore the reality of inequality, discrimination and the imposition of a western model of religiosity the representations of Islam are distorted.

Since September 11 2001 the number and urgency of initiatives that seek to promote positive relationships between religious groups has increased massively. This book shows how attempts to cultivate empathy towards Islam are ineffectual and will remain so until educators engage with the political and policy contexts in which Islam is perceived. As long as educators fail to address the unequal treatment of Muslims by Western society, strategies designed to promote a positive response to Islam will always be compromised.

The book does not champion one representation of Islam over another but raises the question of representation itself as both a modern and a historical process. It explores the different factors that shape that representation in light of the development of a European identity, the changing status of Christianity, and the role of the state after World War Two in its response to ethnicity and race. It argues that education is not aloof from these developments but that these social and historical responses significantly affect how perceptions of Islam in the West are developed and perpetuated.

Many educationists rightly see schools and the curriculum as sites where inequalities and misrepresentations are challenged. Representations in relation to Islam usually appear sympathetic, but we see that they present a world view which is at odds with many popular ideas about Islam. Open a modern textbook designed for primary school children and it will tell you that Islam is a religion of peace. Open the *Daily Mail* and Melanie Phillips will tell you that to refer to Islam as peaceable after the bombings in England in 2005 is a gross self-deception (Phillips, 2005).

This book argues that Orientalist assumptions inform both popular prejudices and many approaches to the teaching of Islam in education. Representations in education are dominated by a multitude of factors and agendas, most of which have very little to do with the activities and beliefs of British Muslims themselves.

Representation and interpretation

At the heart of this book is the recognition that the knowledge about Islam that is presented in education is informed by various political and ideological agendas. The representation of Islam in UK schools, I argue, is shaped by discussions that go well beyond education, to the origins of the notion of 'world religions', multiculturalism and Home Office initiatives.

The representation of Islam in the West is the subject of innumerable debates. Recent studies have looked at how all sections of the media – print, tabloid and broadsheets, documentaries, popular culture and film – have represented Muslims and Islam (Poole, 2000; Ameli, 2007; Bunglawala, 2002; Richardson, 2004).

Although the research often focuses on different aspects of the representation of Islam, the common theme is that Islam is misrepresented. Images in film are often racial and ethnic caricatures (Shaheen, 2003). Islam is presented as inherently prone to violence (Shadid and van Koningsveld, 2001) and many of its beliefs and practices, especially those relating to gender (Ahmed, 1992), are associated with values that are at odds with Western liberalism. Even where the intent is apparently neutral, Islam is nonetheless misrepresented through, for example, assumptions that most Muslims are Arabs, or through a prism that projects a monolithic image of Muslim life (Halliday, 2006). Greaves (2005) maintains that the disparagement of Islam is not limited to the tabloid media but is evident also in the 'academic media' (Greaves, 2005).

Many of the debates about the representation and misrepresentation of Islam are informed by the ideas associated with the work of Edward Said and his arguments in his book, *Orientalism*, most notably that Western portrayals of the Orient in both fact and fiction have created an Orient that exists only in the Western imagination. This Western-created Orient is a false representation, a product of Western colonial thinking and ideology that is essentialised and perpetuated through continued Western domination of the East (Said, 1991).

The premise that the relationship between power and knowledge drives representation is a common theme in many such debates. In their analysis of the representation of Muslims in media, popular culture and policy after 9/11, Ameli and Marandi found that the more statements and representations in the media mirrored dominant Western narratives of Muslims, the more likely were they to be published and reproduced. These authors argue that representation is the result not of a single current in society but of a complex interplay between power structures, the position and aims of minorities and majorities and the ability and power of those actors to act (Ameli and Marandi, 2007).

The educational arena may appear distant from the commercial and populist demand-driven media, but I argue that the representation of Islam which prevails in schools and educational policy is shaped by forces similar to those identified by Ameli and Marandi in their research. The spread of Islamophobia, the rapidly changing policy landscape in education and the international and security focus on Islam all impinge on the representations of Islam in the West.

If we are to understand how Islam is represented in education, it is not enough to transpose Said's analysis onto another scenario such as education. We have to understand what is new, what is specific to contemporary education and what continues from the past. If it is the case that Islam remains the Other then the question is: can that Other be represented fairly? And if so, how?

How this book is organised

Chapter One discusses the dramatic changes in the way Western observers have perceived Islam. It focuses on the way Western ideas about Islam shifted from the belief that Islam was inferior to Christianity as a religion, to its inclusion into the canon of world religions. The chapter looks at the various factors that have influenced the representation of Islam, including the changing relationship between Christianity and national identity, the domination of certain pedagogies, and the key developments in the emergence of Religious Education as a curriculum subject.

Chapter Two argues that the perception of Islam as linked to certain ethnic and religious communities and international developments has affected the status of multicultural policies in the UK. It draws on recent debates about Islam and the limits of multiculturalism and argues that Islam is frequently represented as the embodiment of values that challenge the boundaries of what is acceptable in a western, liberal society. The chapter links this discussion with an emerging consensus among some commentators who believe that multicultural approaches are no longer viable in policy and that new strategies are needed to address diversity and integration.

Chapter Three explores the representation of Islam and Muslims in school textbooks. It considers recent research into the quality, nature and use of textbooks and provides an analysis of the relevant textbooks commonly used in English schools. This review of textbooks and resources covers both historical and recent publications and spans all key stages. It becomes clear that the images and information provided about Islam are often informed by the desire to avoid controversy or to show any aspects of Islam that could be interpreted as illiberal.

Chapter Four provides a detailed analysis of the representation of Islam in current Home Office strategies against terrorism and radicalism, including the initiatives *Prevent* and *REsilience*. The chapter considers the relationship between the agenda of the Home Office regarding security and the context in which Islam is taught in schools. The chapter argues that the desire to counter prejudices and misconceptions against Muslims and Islam, combined with a particular view of Islam promoted by the Home Office, can compromise the way Islam is taught in schools.

Chapter Five argues that the promotion and cultivation in education of tolerance towards Islam can accentuate a perception of 'them and us'. I question the notion of tolerance and propose that if teaching about

Islam fails to acknowledge and challenge Islamophobia and *Orientalism* a flawed and naïve representation of Islam will be perpetuated.

Islam is repeatedly represented in contemporary education as both a subject area and a site of controversy and complexity. Some of these representations appear in textbooks, while others are stated in policies and guidelines. But still more are silently filtered through assumptions that have become an almost naturalised part of the way the Western world sees Islam. The overwhelming impression of these representations is that they are dominated and shaped by agendas and forces that do not originate within Muslim communities.

This book is about how representations of Islam frequently act upon Islam rather than engaging with Muslims and about how education too often fails to challenge this inappropriate approach. It shows how education has often acted as a conduit for the development of ideas that inform and perpetuate Islamophobia and how merely emphasising the positive does nothing to challenge the core of unequal power that shapes representations of Islam in western education.

1

Islam and World Religions

The teacher began the introductory section of the lesson by asking the Year 7 class about important journeys; had they ever been on a really long or important journey? Had anyone in their family ever been on a long journey? What was the most important journey they had ever been on? Did they know what a pilgrimage was and had they ever been on a pilgrimage?

The classroom was especially arranged for the lesson. The desks and chairs were pushed to the sides of the room. Five were left in the middle of the room, placed as far apart from each other as possible and in the middle of each was a set of cards and pictures. The class of 26 boys was divided into groups of four and they visited each table in turn. When each group of boys reached a table they read the cards and looked at the pictures. At some of the tables they mimed or acted out the directions on the cards. At one table, boys pretended to stone the Devil with rocks made out of papier-mâché, and at one stage each group would rush between two of the tables, reenacting Hajar's search for water when she was left in the desert with her young son.

Towards the end of the lesson, the teacher gathered the boys together and recapped the information on the cards and asked some of them to explain the reasons for the actions they had performed at each table. She asked them to consider how they think they would have felt if they really had been throwing stones and rocks at the Devil or if they had been walking round the Kaba with tens of thousands of other pilgrims. The boys were all excited from the activity, the constant movement and negotiation of tables and other boys in such a small space and they were all engaged with the lesson and keen to answer questions. For homework the boys were asked to write a page in answer to one of the following tasks:

- Describe how you think a son would feel about his father taking part in the Hajj when it is so expensive for the family
- Write a journal entry as someone performing Hajj. Remember to explain why Hajj is so important to Muslims
- Write an interview for a newspaper of someone returning from Hajj

This Year 7 lesson in an all boy's school in Kent was part of a half term block of lessons on the Five Pillars of Islam. The boys were introduced to a new Pillar each week and would spend a further two lessons making a poster explaining why the Five Pillars are so important to Muslims. They would be encouraged to use Islamic style calligraphy as part of their design and to avoid the representation of human figures in their drawings. The teacher had planned the lesson with a great deal of care and thought. She believed that active learning was effective, especially with boys, and that it was important for the pupils to get what she called a 'taste' of the physical and communal aspects of Hajj. The idea of getting the boys to mimic the Hajj in her classroom was borrowed from another teacher but she had personally made and laminated all the resources herself. The teacher was aware that Hajj is attended only by Muslims but she believed that her lesson would not cause offence to anyone. She had carefully selected her opening and homework questions so that the class would have opportunities not only to learn about the facts of Hajj but to reflect on the personal and religious meanings that lay behind the rituals.

The teacher was pleased with the lesson; her class were engaged, they did all the activities enthusiastically and they were able to explain why the Hajj was one of the Five Pillars of Islam. Pupils were noisy and excited by the continual rushing from table to table but their comments in the question and answer sessions at the start and end of the lesson showed that they now knew basic facts about Hajj and were aware of some of the economic and spiritual ramifications.

As a lesson on Hajj this scene could be taken as an example of the huge changes both in RE and the teaching of Islam as part of RE in the postwar period. Key features of the lesson mark it out as a modern lesson: it is experiential in parts, it was planned around theories of active learning and, most significantly, the experience of the Hajj, a pilgrimage to Mecca of monumental spiritual significance to Muslims, was presented as a human experience that was accessible to 11 and 12 year old boys. The teacher encouraged pupils to draw parallels between the emotions and feelings of Muslims visiting Mecca and their own excitement about experiences that were important to them. Fifty years ago, the style of the lesson would have been very different and Islam would probably have been referred to as 'Mohammedism'. In the years immediately after the second world war, it is unlikely that Islam would have been included in the curriculum at all.

This chapter looks at the different approaches to teaching Islam in RE in the postwar period. It focuses on the key changes in pedagogy, policy and the philosophies that underpin the development of Islam as a discrete subject area for the curriculum. The chapter examines the process by which Islam made the transition from a religion considered inferior and dangerous to being accepted as part of a canon, one of six world religions. As part of this analysis the chapter questions some aspects of the dominant narratives in the history of RE, especially the way that Islam relates to other religions in the world religions canon. The chapter argues that the negotiation of Islam as a powerful and dynamic force was a major factor in the development of the contemporary model of world religions and that the representation of Islam in the postwar period was framed by the emergence of a phenomenological definition of religion.

The simplest history of RE is based on a narrative that starts with confessional religious instruction and ends with a model of RE that is objective, liberal and committed to a world religions approach. In this story the trajectory is a liberal journey from an overtly confessional approach to Christianity to one where the six world religions are taught without bias and pupils are encouraged to empathise with all religions equally.

3

The story begins in the time before significant immigration, when the UK was mostly white and Christian and the teaching of religion in schools was no more than the 'missionary wing of the Christian churches' (Wright and Brandon, 2000:1). Religious Instruction was confessional; its rationale was built on the assumption that the Christian parents of children desired schools to nurture their children into the Christian faith: the teaching of religion in the classroom was an adjunct to learning in the Sunday School. In this history there was a rupture that challenged the legitimacy of confessional Christian education caused by dramatic changes in demographics and the religious sensibilities of an entire nation. This narrative describes how the twin factors of increased diversity due to immigration and the parallel decline in Church attendance and belief combined to prompt a rethinking of the content, rationale and approach to the teaching of religion in community schools.

Two pieces of research are often cited as providing the theoretical justification for the remodelling of religion in education. In 1961, Harold Loukes published his research into what he called 'the new frontier in education'. The frontier he was referring to was between a generation of young people who are unchurched and ignorant of the main beliefs and practices of Christianity and a society that wishes its young to be schooled in Christianity but is itself secular (Loukes, 1961:8). As part of his research he visited secondary schools and conducted discussions with teenagers about a range of issues including the relevance of Christianity, the state of the church and the place of morals in a modern society. Loukes argued that this 'most questioning and determined of generations' were asking questions that deserved serious answers from their educators. When teenagers asked 'Why should I be a Christian if I can be good without?' or 'How far is it right for Christians to impose their beliefs on others?' they were raising issues that went beyond the boundaries of traditional confessional religious instruction. Loukes argued that just as children need to be made ready for reading so they need to be made ready for religion. Rather than instruct young children into Christianity, they could be brought towards Christianity through acts of love and care. This was still a model of religious education that was founded on a belief in Christianity but it was one that recognised the pressures and influence of secular society and provided an educa-

4

tional rationale for a distancing from explicit Christian instruction (Bates, 1984).

Ronald Goldman provided research that explained the lack of religious engagement of young people and children in the context of contemporary theories of child development. Goldman believed that his research, where he asked children to respond to three Bible stories and three religious pictures, proved that children were cognitively unprepared to understand religious concepts before they reached a certain age. He used a Piagetian model of child development to explain how before a certain age it was unlikely that a child could engage meaningfully with the theology underpinning Bible stories (Goldman, 1968).

Although the robustness of the research and conclusions of both these writers has been questioned (Bates, 1984), their work is significant because they provided the basis for a rewriting of confessional education. The conclusions drawn from these projects, along with the growth of immigrant populations, underpinned a withdrawal from confessional Christian instruction and a move towards an RE that was child-centered, creative and objective. More importantly, this period heralded a world religions approach built on phenomenological principles.

The story of Islam in RE is in part the story of RE. In line with the narrative just described, Islam would have had no place in the teaching of religion until the 1960s, apart from the few schools where it was taught as part of a unit on comparative religions, and then only in the upper school. It was only when world religions were incorporated into the seminal Birmingham Agreed Syllabus in 1975 that Islam was officially recognised within compulsory education as part of the canon of world religions alongside Christianity, Buddhism, Sikhism, Judaism and Hinduism. In 1988, the Education Reform Act gave further recognition to Islam within education by acknowledging it as one of the principal religions of England.

This is a seductive narrative. It suggests that RE has been a part of a progressive liberal trend within education, and that accusations of indoctrination are a thing of the past. In this scenario RE has successfully distanced itself from confessional models in community schools and it has effectively positioned itself as an innovator in the teaching of diversity and tolerance. It is, however, a flawed and incomplete narrative that

5

is at best oversimplified but at worst perpetuates an uncritically benign image of RE in relation to the understanding and negotiation of racial and religious difference in education.

A full history of RE or one that focuses on the treatment of a single religion cannot possibly be encompassed in a single chapter. Others have noted that attempts at providing such a history have failed to take full account of the complexity of the factors and political and social contexts in which RE has evolved (Parker and Freathy, 2011). This chapter focuses on a single issue: the evolution of Islam into a curriculum subject area. It examines the history of Islam in RE through tracing the roots of the idea of world religions and the development of approaches grounded in multi-faith and intercultural approaches to the teaching of religion. I argue that changes in the way Islam has been understood and presented in the fields of anthropology, theology, religious studies and education were often grounded in the negotiation a of nineteenth century European identity and the changing status of Christianity in the postwar years.

Why world religions?

That there are six world religions is a mantra that runs through every textbook on RE and every agreed syllabus. It is almost impossible to find books written for children or young people on any religion that is not one of the designated six. Books for young teenagers on religion are almost completely confined to those six exam topic religions. Islam is frequently described as the fastest growing religion in the world, the second largest religion in the world and as a religion whose significance goes beyond the spiritual and has geopolitical importance. Today, it seems self-evident that Islam should claim a place on the curriculum but a generation ago such a claim would not have been made. A second unquestioned assumption in the UK is that where Islam appears in the curriculum, it is presented as a religious tradition and should therefore be governed by the same curriculum regulations and pedagogies as inform the teaching of other religions. The impact of the second of these assumptions is examined in Chapter Five but the status of Islam as a particular type of religion, a world religion, is a key factor in understanding the process by which Islam came to be included in the curriculum. This process was not merely one of inclusion but laid the basis for a future representation of Islam in the curriculum characterised by a sense of Othering and difference.

As a tutor in Religious Education, I often ask student teachers where they think the idea comes from that there are six world religions and their answers are sometimes surprising. The most common explanation is that the religions claim their place in the canon because they are the biggest and most influential religions in the world. Another common explanation is that they are there because of their relationship to western civilisation or because they were once religions of the empire. Many students argue that other traditions (Confucianism, animism, shamanism, to name a few) are not real religions, describing them variously as cultural practices or ways of life. When asked to explain why a practice like animism, which is found in every continent, is never normally covered in RE lessons, students often explain that its lack of structure or core rituals, the absence of sacred texts, priesthood or places of worship mean that it is too amorphous to be included in a curriculum and too disparate a practice to be considered a discrete body of knowledge.

The question of where this canon came from or even the legitimacy of the canon itself is rarely addressed in RE, even though as a paradigm it has come under systematic criticism for many years in other disciplines (Owen, 2011). Even where RE specialists have questioned the validity of models of religiosity that project clearly defined traditions or a historical understanding of concepts of religion (Jackson, 1995), this discourse has had no significant impact on the way religions are represented in textbooks or the agreed syllabi. Agreed syllabi and the majority of RE textbooks assume that world religions exist, that there are normally six of them and that they rightly constitute the bedrock of an education in religion. Yet the single question, 'Why are world religions the basis of non-confessional RE?' throws a critical light on a number of key moments in the history of RE, not least the circumstances that lead to Islam being recognised as a world religion. The question is not merely a matter of historical curiosity but one that bears on contemporary practice in RE because the unquestioned acceptance of world religions in textbooks and agreed syllabi influences the perception of Islam as well as the relationship between Islam and other religions.

In his comprehensive history of RE in England and Wales, Terence Copley warns that too often the beginnings of contemporary RE are located in the 1944 Education Act. He is keen to draw our attention to later developments, especially the 1988 Education Reform Act (Copley, 2003). But to fully grasp the significance and origins of world religions and to appreciate the significance of the inclusion of Islam in this category we need to look at Christianity not merely as a subject in the curriculum but also at the relationship between Christianity and the nation.

Empire and the invention of world religions

That Britain ruled an empire and that the nation and its empire were Christian were unquestioned facts in the nineteenth century. There was an assumed relationship between the power and the truth of Christianity. The success of empire gave a glory and a suggestion of superiority to Christianity and the work of missionaries was not an adjunct to imperial domination but a seamless part of Britain's control and expansion of empire (Stanley, 1990). The assumption that the civilising nature of Christianity justified Britain's conquest and domination was mirrored in the conviction that to be white, British and Christian was to belong to the most superior race in the world (Johnston, 2003). Empire Day was celebrated in schools across the Empire. Children would salute the flag, sing patriotic songs and perhaps black up and perform plays that retold the adventures of British heroes like Clive of India, exemplifying the bond between Christianity and nationhood (Heater, 2001).

The intimate relationship between Christianity and Empire makes the eventual journey to a world religions approach astounding. What makes the transition even more dramatic is the inclusion of Islam as a part of that canon. Fred Halliday argues that even before the creation of the British Empire and after the development of a Western European identity, the limits of Empire and of Europe were defined by Islam. While western scholars, traders and explorers had to discover other cultures and beliefs, Muslim societies have been neighbours with Christians for at least 1200 years. Buddhism, Hinduism, Jainism and Sikhism were unknown to Western scholars until imperial domination brought them to their attention. But Islam was not a distant and unknown phenomenon; it has been an intimate part of European and British history since before the crusades. As Halliday notes, for at least a thousand years where colonies, empire and Europe ended Islam began. In Africa, in India and in Europe itself 'it is a strategic reality that it is the Islamic peoples who constitute the outer boundaries of Europe, forming a vast semi-circle that abuts onto the lands to the south and the east' (Halliday, 1995:71).

The hostile, aggressive response of many nineteenth century western writers to the 'vast semi-circle of Islam' around them is well documented. Islam was disparaged and belittled and was misrepresented in European texts for two hundred years (Jonker and Thobani, 2010). How is it then that Islam was incorporated into the world religions model, a model that appears to presents six religions on an equal platform? The significance of world religions as the basis for contemporary RE is generally recognised (Geaves, 1998) and, while there are different interpretations as to when and why this happened, a common theme in many of the theories is that the modern idea of religion is rooted in the meeting point between western intellectuals, colonialists and indigenous peoples. This meeting point is invariably characterised by an unequal relationship where western scholars articulate a desire to see all other practices through the lens of Christianity or to reaffirm the superiority of Christianity (Geaves, 1998).

Robert Jackson argues that concepts of 'religions' and 'religion' 'that are generally accepted uncritically by recent and contemporary religious educators' are relatively modern and contestable (Jackson, 1995). He locates the origins of the concept of religion as a discrete entity in two complimentary developments: first, the process of defining other religions from Christianity as part of the unequal power relationship between colonisers and the colonised and, second, the emergence of the idea that religion has an essence.

The different ways of conceiving what we know today as Islam are mirrored up to the end of the nineteenth century by the many names non-Muslims used to refer to followers of Islam: the Saracens, the Tartars, Turks, the Mohammedans, Musulmans and Muhammadanism (Smith, 1978). In his analysis of the circumstances that heralded world religions, Dennis Bates argues that the origins of comparative religion are located in the new science of religion that developed in the late

9

nineteenth century. Scholars not of theology but of philology and anthropology engaged with the discoveries of traditions and cultures new to the West through the work of F. Max Muller and Frazer and created the entirely new subject areas of the history of religions or comparative religions. Bates presents a scenario where contact with sacred texts and practices of other faiths in the context of new ideas about evolution meant that the universality of religion as a human experience was recognised, with Christianity conceived as the pinnacle of that experience (Bates, 1994).

The American Professor of European Intellectual History, Tomoko Masuzawa, gives a significantly more radical analysis of how world religions evolved. She argues that the world religions approach was attractive to Western thinkers precisely because religions were not considered to be equal to one another. World religions, as originally conceived, elevated Christianity as the only truly universal religion in that canon. It was only possible to do this through the systematic representation of Islam and Judaism as non-universal religions. Like Bates, she identifies the origins of an intellectual and social climate that recognised the existence and even the significance of other systems of belief in the mid to late nineteenth century. Her theory, however, rests on a broader political analysis of the relationship between national identity and intellectual discovery. Her argument is that before the eighteenth century the notion of religion as we employ the term today, with its 'sense of objective reality, concrete facticity, and utter self-evidence' (Masuzawa, 2005:2) did not exist and that its development is intertwined with the emergence of a distinctive Western identity.

This Western identity was forged at a time when imperial nations were at their height and were conscious of the immensity of the world population that was neither like them nor controlled by them (Hobson, 2004). Their modern concept of religion was, as Bates describes, of beliefs and practices that could be characterised as a universal experience. The creation of a canon was both a response to the recognition of other systems of belief and the creation of a lens that privileged Christianity and preserved their superiority.

The process by which the canon of world religions was created was not by means of a series of gentle intellectual discussions between European academics but came about after a tumultuous period in the Christian West of self doubt and reflection (Hastings, 1987). It has become a fundamental assumption of modern RE that there are religions with as many or more members than Christianity, which are more dynamic, have created sublime works of art and developed moral codes. For many Victorians, these ideas would have been shocking. In the mid-nineteenth century, the questioning of the position of Christianity was radical and disturbing for a nation underpinned by the assumption that their control of the world's greatest empire was founded on its being a Christian empire (Mehta, 1999). Nineteenth century recognition of a canon of great world religions, of which Christianity was only one, necessitated the painful acknowledgement that Christianity and, by implication, Western civilisation was not the sole source of temporal power or spiritual authority.

Mid-nineteenth century intellectual debate on the nature of religion and especially the relationship between Christianity and Islam was characterised by a tension caused by the desire to reaffirm the superiority of Christianity and the recognition that Islam was a dynamic and powerful force in the world. This tension is illustrated in the public lectures on 'Faiths of the World' held at Edinburgh Cathedral in 1882. The lecture on 'Mahommedanism' by the Reverend James Cameron Lees described in hushed and awed tones the sight of a Muslim praying in a mosque where 'a thousand people before him' will all be buried 'in profound silence'. He admonished his listeners for using the term Mahommedanism when Islam 'is the more correct designation'. However, his main point was that Islam poses a political, social and religious challenge to the Empire:

> Mahommedanism has carved its name deep on the history of the world; nor can we feel sure it has played its part. It is here with us still – a powerful faith, commanding the bigoted allegiance of 175,000,000 souls, 40,000,000 of whom are our own fellow subjects, presenting on its political side in Turkey, India, Africa, problems most difficult of solution; a religion adding to its adherents by an unceasing proselytism. ... (Lees, 1882:363)

In 1853, Fredrick Denison Maurice was deprived of his professorships of Divinity and English Literature at King's College, London, charged with the crime of heterodoxy. His great offence was not that he was a leading Christian Socialist and had founded the Working Men's College in 1854, or that he championed the education of women (he founded the Working Women's College in 1879), but that he argued that all religious systems that survived and prospered did so because they contained a portion of truth if not the whole truth. He had been invited to give the 1854 Boyle public lectures on *The Religions of the World: and their Relations to Christianity*, and he took the opportunity not merely to gently admonish his listeners for their ignorance in repeatedly referring to the religion of the Mussulmen as Mahometanism but to remind them that when Christians engage with Mussulmen they must be ready to acknowledge that their desire for truth, the source of beauty and the living God was as authentic as their own (Maurice, 1861).

The Victorian awareness of Islam as a competing dynamic force was to have a lasting impact on the development of a model of world religions. Islam could not be dismissed. Its authority and influence needed to be addressed, but in a context where the status of Christianity was reaffirmed rather than challenged. This was a process that rested on what Masuzawa refers to as 'a dramatic transformation of Europe's relation to the rest of the world' (Masuzawa, 2005:180).

Before European modernity much of the world was Islamic. The advent of European modernity demanded restructuring European self-understanding and reimagining the Muslim world to allow European powers to represent themselves as the pinnacle of civilisation. This was done by presenting a European identity that was intertwined with modernity and universal principles while all other traditions were tied to specific racial or ethnic identities or else presented as historical precursors to Christianity itself. Distance was created between Christianity and the religions that shared its monotheism and prophetic traditions: Islam and Judaism. Judaism was presented as an older, underdeveloped and limited universalism, Islam as ethnically tied to the Arabs, unable to break away from its Semitic roots and characterised by a renegade universalism.

In contemporary RE, the concept of world religion appears as either a purely descriptive phrase or a concept that allows a plural consideration of religious difference. The origins of the term are not, however, rooted in the desire for a model that would allow an equitable consideration of religions, but in the evolution of a European identity positioned at the peak of human development and spirituality. Islam has a key part in this canon not because it is a religion equal in every respect to Christianity but because its portrayal as an ethnically specific religion, one that is superficially monotheistic but actually tied to the practices and preoccupations of the Arabs, served to throw the universal aspirations of Christianity into sharp relief.

How did a concept that was premised on the assumption of the privileging of Christianity to the detriment of other religions, especially Islam, come to be the bedrock of contemporary RE? The classic history of RE in this period is Terence Copley's *Teaching Religion: Fifty years of religious education in England and Wales* (2003). Copley charts the complex shifts and accommodations made by academics, a Christian establishment and educationalists as they vied to be the chief architects of religion in a modern curriculum (Copley, 2003). Although his history provides a broad view of the recent period, he rarely includes discussion of one of the most important reasons for the place of Islam in RE: the increasing racial and ethnic diversity of the UK. This chapter goes on to explain how racial diversity, combined with an elevated fear of dogmatism and confessionalism on behalf of Christian stakeholders in education, led to a world religions approach to the study of religion in schools that once again maintained a dominant Christian presence in a plural context.

RE in postwar Britain

Islam played no real part in the education of young people and children until 1969. The world religions approach was first promoted by a working party of academics and educationalists interested in the relationship between the study of comparative religions and school. Robert Jackson argues that the term may have originated as a synonym for 'religions of the world' and distinguished between the 'living religions of the world' and religions which did not have a universal mission (Jackson, 1999). However, it was the impact of the Shap working party that embedded the term in educational practice. Its conferences and discussions were as influential as any of the key pieces of legislation on religion in schools and its impact is still evident today in the dominant approaches to Islam as a curriculum subject.

Many authors look back to the postwar period as a golden age of Christian instruction in schools (Bates, 1996). No religions other than Christianity were taught except on rare occasions in sixth form lessons. Where Islam did appear it was taught in comparison to Christianity and usually in such a way as to demonstrate the superiority of Christian beliefs and practices. Islam was commonly referred to as Mohammedanism, and its key beliefs and practices were often explained as derivative of Christian thought (Thobani, 2010).

Religions apart from Christianity were unfavourably depicted, and given a hierarchical order. Religions associated with 'lower cultures' were taught as spiritually stunted forms of religiosity, representing a less evolved form of religious feeling. Islam was normally considered a higher religion but it was frequently placed below Buddhism. We see this in *Comparative Religion* by J. E. Carpenter, which was reprinted five times between 1913 and 1937. Buddhism is presented as a religion that sprung out of a 'moral revolt' against the domination of the Brahman, so that Buddhism is portrayed as a universal spiritual impulse. In contrast, the origins of Islam are presented in the context of materialistic and political intrigue characterised by self-interested speculation (Carpenter, 1913).

How the world religions canon, and Islam as a part of that canon, came to be adopted by RE has to be understood in the context of the state of postwar Christianity. This period may have been dominated by confessional Christian teaching, in a time that Copley describes as shaped by the assumption that church, nation and education shared the same interests but was a period of crisis for Christianity, in education and as a whole. In his last book, *Indoctrination, Education and God* (2005), Copley provided a harsh polemic against the domination of liberal values in education that permitted nothing less than the indoctrination of young people into secular truths and dispositions. His argument was that the twentieth century saw the gradual erosion of Christian practices including church attendance, Sunday closing and religious broadcasting and that Christian morality declined as a result. In the scenario he paints, liberal and secular forces eroded the Christian fabric of British culture and contributed to the view of teachers, families and pupils alike that confessional Christian education was inappropriate, redundant and unwelcome.

The increasing secularism of society is usually cited as one of the main contributory factors in the erosion of Christian practices in England. The collapse of Christian authority heralded new approaches to religion in education. The immediate postwar period saw a growing recognition that the type of biblical studies that dominated most religion teaching in schools appeared irrelevant to many teachers and pupils (Jackson, 2004). The growth of secularism is usually given as the source of this irrelevance (Davie, 2007) and this period was informed by a desire to make religion seem more relevant and less dogmatic too. Edwin Cox, in *Changing Aims in Religious Education* (1966), describes a situation where religion has so little practical influence on present day life that many parents think that the time could be more productively spent on a 'more utilitarian subject' (Cox, 1966:9). Attempts to make the teaching of religion more meaningful for pupils and which acknowledged that families were less likely to be religious appeared more credible in the light of Goldman and Loukes's research.

While it is true that the Churches experienced a dramatic decline and that Christian presence in the public sphere diminished, it would be misleading to attribute the victory of liberal values simply to the fact that they were more attractive to a postwar generation because they were more convenient. In many respects, it was the divisions within Christianity, and the fact that many perceived the authority of Christianity after the war to be compromised, that accelerated the growth and influence of liberalism (Badham, 1989) This was a time when many Christian thinkers were uncertain about the authority of the Church and when the relevance of Christianity was questioned with as much thoroughness by those inside the Church as outside (Marwick, 2003). From the end of the Second World War to the start of the 1960s, debates in education were characterised by questions of how best to maintain an approach to education that would bring children closer to (a Christian) God (Copley, 2005). But in the context of declining church attendance and greater liberalism, the very nature of Christian education appeared problematic.

So why was a world religions approach not adopted in the immediate aftermath of the Second World War? The answer lies in the extent to which England remained wedded to Christian culture in the years following the war. The 1944 Education Act not only envisioned a major role for RE in the reconstruction of society but intended it to aid the recovery of the specifically Christian roots of society (Wright, 2007). This left no place in education for any religion other than Christianity. Any approach that did not aim to nurture Christianity would have been unthinkable. The world religions approach to education only became a possibility once the reality of Christian education had died, as it had done by the early 1960s (Copley, 2005). Even then, the introduction of world religions was a struggle and was only accepted when it was incorporated with an approach that safeguarded Christianity (and other religions) from debates about truth claims in the classroom (Thobani, 2010).

Shap and the reframing of Islam as a world religion

The development of Comparative Religion as a subject in universities provided the basis for the introduction of world religions into the RE curriculum and the reframing of Christianity and other religions into what would now be called world religion. Debates over the most effective ways to study religion were as rife in universities as they were in schools but the approach that dominated was one that advocated professional impartiality. Some academics argued that this distance was not appropriate to the study of religion and would prevent students from engaging with religious ideas or experiences and truth claims (eg. Reno, 1979), but it was this very feature that made the phenomenological approach so well suited for the teaching of religions in schools. While it is simplistic to imply curriculum design merely mirrored theoretical developments (Parker and Freathy, 2011), an understanding of the way religiosity was theorised may offer some insight into the way religions were packaged as curriculum subjects.

In 1969 a working party made up of academics in comparative religion, lecturers in education and teachers met to develop materials and an understanding of the issues relating to religion in schools that was premised on a world religions approach. In her history of the Shap working party, Mary Hayward describes how some members of the group had never 'encountered' other religions before (Hayward, 2008). Nonetheless, there was a real passion amongst its members to provide the training, resources and dispositions that would enable the six world religions to be taught to all ages. Their approach discouraged a questioning of truth claims and resulted in the presentation of those religions in particular and fixed categories. This meant that caricatures of these religions were unlikely to be challenged in the classroom.

This philosophy was most closely associated with the work of Ninian Smart. Smart established the first department of Religious Studies in a British university and his approach was aimed at achieving an emphatic awareness of many religions through the bracketing out of prejudices and preconceptions (Bates, 1996). In *Secular Education and the Logic of Religion*, Smart introduced a typology of religion that identified six features – myths, rituals, social forms, experiences, doctrines and ethics – which he maintained were found in all religions (Smart, 1968). Smart advocated an approach that rejected Christian evangelism or confessionalism in schools and which encouraged pupils to develop empathy in relation to religion (Rankin, 1993).

The approach championed by the Shap working party was not automatically accepted by schools or by some Christian educationalists who still sought to develop a model of Christian education that would be relevant and attractive to pupils. Thobani describes the period as characterised by a fierce struggle between liberal Protestant educators, secular humanists and a conservative establishment (Thobani, 2010). But in retrospect, it is possible to understand why it became the bedrock underpinning most contemporary pedagogies of RE because, while it insisted on rejecting a confessional approach to the teaching of Christianity, at the same time it illegitimated any approach to the teaching of religion that was critical. The uncritical nature of the world religions paradigm may have been the subject of a great deal of criticism in Religious Studies (McCutcheon, 2001), but it is precisely this quality that made it so attractive to educationalists. What the approach articulated through Shap and the Schools Council Working Paper 36, *Religious Education in Secondary Schools* (1971) did was to replace the 'intellectual and cultic indoctrination' associated with confessional teaching with a philosophy that promoted a phenomenological framework to the teaching of religion in schools. Their work provided an educational rationale for a model of teaching of religion in schools that was not directly linked with Christian nurture.

Smart's influence had another profound and lasting impact on the way religions were conceived as world religions. His dimensional typology based on aspects of religion that are common to all religions meant that all religions were conceptualised within that framework. Smart probably never intended that his typology should be adopted as a rigid conceptual framework for all religions, or that it should act as a template that excluded approaches to the study of religion that were based on cultural or social interpretations (Barnes, 2007). Yet the pervasive use of headings and topics derived from Smart's typology dominate nearly every agreed syllabus. In effect, Smart created a model for defining religion so that every religion in RE can be understood and studied using the same categories.

A review of the guidelines presented through the Schools Council Project on Religious Education in two of its handbooks for teachers shows how Smart's typology was adapted to an approach that could be used in schools. Published in 1977, *Journeys into Religion* was written as a handbook for teachers, as part of the Religious Education in Secondary Schools Project. The first part introduces the teacher to the principles underpinning the recommended units, including a critique of the then dominant approach to RE and a rejection of a pedagogy that assumes 'Christianity is a right and proper part of the school curriculum in a Christian society' (Schools Council, 1977:9). It goes on to define religion as a combination of six dimensions and stresses that religion is more than just a collection of rituals with associated moral teachings.

The section on Islam, *The Muslim way of life*, is included in the recommendations for pupils aged 11 and 12. A number of features would be unusual today. The most striking feature of the unit is the range and depth of the recommended readings and resources for teachers. Teachers are encouraged to read books on the origins of Islam, on Muslim countries and texts produced by the Muslim Educational Trust. Also unusual is the presumption throughout that children will be studying the lives and beliefs of Muslims in their social context. In the section on *Islam in Britain* pupils are to learn about Zakat (the fourth pillar of Islam) but also about how Muslims live their lives in different communities in the UK.

The use of world religions as a category to define religions and the teaching of religions means that as subjects in the curriculum they are regulated first by the assumptions that originally created the category and secondly by the demands of a non-confessional educational environment. This meant that within school-based education Islam was to be forever framed within a prism that first positioned it against Christianity as a lower form of monotheism (Thobani, 2010). Secondly it meant that a generation of school children would compare sacred books, rituals and places of worship without ever having to consider the social context of Islam. The decontextualised and abstracted Islam of world religions is maintained through numerous agreed syllabi and thousands of specially written textbooks, as discussed in Chapter Three.

One defence of the world religion paradigm could be that despite its flaws it does have the merit of treating all religions equally. Although this claim can be disputed (see Bolton, 1993), there is a far more significant question for the representation of Islam in education: Islam was not just one of six world religions; it was the religion which confronted Christianity on a global scale and which challenged Christian claims to universalism. The remoulding of the world's religions in the image of Western, Europeanised Christianity diminishes all religions but it could be argued that the illusion of uniformity promoted by the world religions paradigm affects Islam most of all precisely because Islam was, and remains, such a dynamic force in the modern world. The next chapter explores further developments in RE in education and how they, too, impact disproportionately on the teaching of Islam. It also looks at how contemporary developments and relationships with Islam have, in turn, left their marks on the curriculum.

2

The limits of multiculturalism

I n 2011, at an international conference on security in Munich, Prime Minister David Cameron announced that 'state multiculturalism' was dead. He argued for 'a much more active, muscular liberalism' where common values would take precedence over the recognition of difference (Cameron, 2011). The Prime Minister was not discussing educational or liberal strategies *per se*, neither was he talking about the general promotion of values in schools and elsewhere – he was talking about Islam. In his speech he claimed that multiculturalism was discredited because it led to the fostering of separate cultures rather than the celebration of common shared values. It was clear he was again referring to the perceived refusal of certain minority communities, especially Muslims, to integrate or to move beyond being defined by religion and ethnicity. That he should publically discuss an issue concerning British Muslims and domestic policy at an international security conference revealed how he, like many, links the dangers associated with radical Islam with the perceived failure of multiculturalism.

Cameron clearly believed Islam was responsible for the death of multiculturalism. His Munich speech generated anger and opposition from defenders of multiculturalism and some Muslim groups but discussions about the credibility of multiculturalism and the role of Islam in its demise have been gaining ground for some time. In 2004, the Chair of the Commission for Racial Equality, Trevor Phillips had stated that 'multiculturalism suggests separateness' and argued that instead of celebrating a multitude of cultures we should be pursuing a common, shared culture with common values. 'Our ideal,' he said, 'should be one nation of many faces; one culture integrating many faiths and traditions'. He argued that the huge response he had provoked was a debate 'waiting to happen' and that anti-racists needed to recognise that multiculturalism had become a 'sleight of hand' where politicians could dance the night away at 'Asian events' but fail to oversee an equal distribution of grants (Phillips, 2004). The public criticism of multicultural education by someone so closely associated with racial equality marked a new stage in the attacks on multiculturalism as a tool for negotiating diversity and inequality. Previously, most critiques of multiculturalism had come either from the right, which saw any recognition of practices and traditions that were avowedly 'not British' as undermining British values, or from the left, which mocked multicultural education as a sop to genuine anti-racist education (Troyna, 1983). Phillips' comments marked the beginning of the attack on multiculturalism and a focus instead on Islam.

This chapter examines the way Islam is represented in multiculturalism in education and especially in RE, and asks why Islam has been blamed for its failure. It discusses the relationship between the development of a visible and articulate Muslim identity in the UK and a growing consensus that it is no longer possible to accommodate Islam within a multicultural framework. I argue that there is a relationship between the development of an approach to race and ethnicity based on the premise that communities should integrate and embrace a common set of values, and the representation of Muslim communities as resistant to integration.

The birth of multiculturalism

Acknowledgement of racial inequality and the contribution of minority groups to the UK has always been an uneven and ambiguous feature of educational policy and curriculum content. The presence, however, of an ever-increasing black and Asian population has had a huge impact on the teaching of religion in schools and the pedagogies which underpin it. The postwar period was a time of intense and explicit racism in education. The arrival of immigrants from the commonwealth was often met with hostility. In his review of the racialisation of the curriculum at this time, Mike Cole tells how in the early 1960s white parents in Southall, London, complained to the Minister of Education that there were too many immigrant children in schools. The government insti-gated a policy where immigrant children were bussed to schools in the suburbs to restrict the numbers to no more than 30 per cent in any one school (Cole, 2012).

The story is interesting not only as a graphic example of the hostility shown to immigrants and their children, but because it illustrates the assumptions held about the way immigrants were expected to relate to their new home at the time. It was expected that immigrants would assimilate as quickly as possible and that embracing the customs and values of Britain would be an unproblematic and positive process. A British style of life could be achieved as soon as migrants learnt English and adopted English customs. The Education Department of Birming-ham University set up the first department for teaching English as a second language in 1960, and Edge Hill College in Lancashire intro-duced the first teacher training course for teaching immigrant children. These measures were designed to meet the needs of communities who were barred from integration and participation because of their lan-guage.

Although racism in the form of attacks, discrimination against people from immigrant backgrounds in employment and immigration visas was endemic in Britain during the 1960s and '70s (Bhat, Carr-Hill and Ohri, 1990), education did not concern itself about racial discrimina-tion or inequality of treatment because of race. The decades from the 1950s through to the end of the '70s in education were characterised by neglect, colour blindness and ineffectual tinkering (Gillborn, 2008).

In the 1970s black and Asian communities began to demand better edu-cation for their children (Cole, 2012), but it was their frustration and rage that forced schools and politicians to address race as an urgent issue. Riots in 1981 in London, Birmingham, Liverpool, Manchester, Coventry and Leeds broke out after police launched 'Operation Swamp' to check the immigration status of black people in London. In 1985, there were further disturbances in London and Birmingham. The flashpoints dif-fered, and in different areas various ethnic groups were involved, but the impact was the same. There followed recognition that racial divisions in society had to be addressed and that previous policies had failed.

One of the striking aspects of the discussion of the riots was the focus on young people's behaviour, not just during the riots but also in schools. Black and Asian children were characterised differently: black pupils were more likely to be portrayed as violent and disruptive, while Asian pupils were presented as passive and quiet. All debates about race and ethnicity during the 1980s routinely referred to the two groups in this way (Tomlinson, 1983). Remarkably, there was no mention of Muslim pupils. During the 1970s, the Department of Education published several important reports, including *The Education of Immigrants, Education Survey 13* (in 1971) and *Education in Schools: a Consultative Document* (in 1977) that considered the education of children from immigrant families but none mentioned Islam or Muslim children.

Little and Willey's report *Multi Ethnic Britain: The Way Forward*, published by the Schools Council Project in 1981, assessed the state of training, resources and provision for the education of pupils from black and Asian families. It discussed the progress of ethnic minority children and the provision for West Indian children but made no mention of Muslim children or Muslim communities. Islam and Muslims are invisible in these documents not because the Asian communities mentioned in the reports did not include Muslims, but because their religion was not perceived as a significant aspect of their identity.

The explosion of urban unrest, however, and the growing demand within education circles for acceptance of the need to tackle racial inequality, prompted a number of reports that officially recognised the disadvantage experienced by black and Asian children. In 1979, the government commissioned the Rampton Report (1981) to look at the education of West Indian children and in 1985 the Swann report *Education for All* was published. *Education for All* spearheaded the embedding of ideas associated with multiculturalism into all areas of education over the next decade.

In 1982 approximately 20 LEAs had written multicultural policies and by 1986 there were over one hundred (Tomlinson, 2008). Over the next twenty years, Gillborn (2008) found there was a creeping acceptance that many children from black and Asian backgrounds had experienced inequality in education and that schools had a responsibility to confront inequality and to address their own role in the perpetuation of racial discrimination. Gillborn describes this as a period when educa-tion became an important arena for anti-racist debate and where anti-racism came to denote a series of practices to counter racial discrimina-tion (Gillborn, 2008).

The Stephen Lawrence Inquiry, published in 1999, exposed the racism in the police force and other public bodies. Institutional racism became part of the language in debates about race and education, even if it was not accepted by all (Parsons, 2008). There has never been a consensus among educationalists about the effectiveness or legitimacy of multi-culturalism in education (Brandt, 1986; Tomlinson, 1996), but it was the approach favoured by the schools and the LEAs which tried to tackle inequality. However, even this was limited (Tomlinson, 1996).

As long ago as 1974, the DES reported that 'too many' entrants to the teaching profession did not have enough experience or understanding of a multiracial, multicultural society (DES, 1977) and there was very little training for teachers to address this (Townsend and Brittan, 1972). This is still the case today.

Despite the absence of systematic training and support for teachers in multicultural education, the 1980s and '90s saw what Tomlinson calls an 'outpouring of literature and comment' from academic, policy, prac-tical and political sources (Tomlinson, 2008:92) in relation to multi-cultural and anti-racist education. The impact of this outpouring was negligible in terms of practice but ideas of multiculturalism as an ap-proach to ethnic and racial differences in schools became the norm (Modood, 2010). The Education Reform Act of 1988, which established the framework for the National Curriculum, did not prioritise issues of race and racism, but did use the language of multiculturalism (Gillborn, 1995) and teachers and educationalists who were concerned with the experiences of black and Asian pupils similarly used the language of multiculturalism to describe their strategies in the classroom.

In 1984, in an article for the conservative journal *The Salisbury Review*, Bradford head teacher Ray Honeyford blamed multiculturalism in edu-cation for the failure of immigrant families and their children to inte-grate fully into British society. It showed how firmly multiculturalism had become synonymous with antiracism that he chose to attack multi-culturalism (Hardy and Vieler-Porter, 1992). Mrs Thatcher later invited the by then sacked Honeyford to attend an educational seminar at 10 Downing Street on the future of education, thereby officially signalling Conservative distaste of multiculturalism.

Religious Education is one area where the aims of multiculturalism were accepted enthusiastically. The teachers' acceptance of multiculturalism as a positive strategy against discrimination and inequality, the recognition that inequality exists and could possibly lead to social unrest, contributed to the evolution of RE as the primary educational arena in multicultural education.

RE and multiculturalism

It is noteworthy that the late 1970s and early 1980s, when antiracist education and the growth of multiculturalism was most recognised in education (Tomlinson, 2008), was also the time which Grimmitt (2010) identifies as the most productive in the promotion of secular models of RE. It would be impossible to understand the development of RE as a curriculum area without understanding the ideas underpinning the growth of multiculturalism at this time.

RE has situated itself as a tool for the development of positive attitudes towards difference since it embraced a world religions model of religiosity. The Swann Report (DES, 1985) specifically identified a role for RE in preparing pupils for life in a multicultural society and this aim persists in agreed syllabi across the country as well as in the current Non-Statutory National Framework for Religious Education (NSFRE). The NSFRE explicitly defines RE as a curriculum area that promotes specific values and whose contribution to pupil learning lies in the creation of desirable attitudes, including respecting difference and challenging prejudice and stereotyping (QCA, 2004:9).

Reviewing twenty agreed syllabi from a variety of LEAs, I found that every one identifies the positive role that RE can play as a facilitator of positive attitudes towards difference as a key rationale for its place in the school curriculum. For example, the most recent Wakefield syllabus states that 'RE enables pupils to develop respect for and sensitivity towards others .... It promotes discernment and enables pupils to combat prejudice' (Wakefield, 2007:6). The syllabus for Devon, Plymouth and Torbay situates its provision for RE within the needs of the Every Child

Matters policy and argues that RE has a role to play in dispelling the prejudices and stereotypes perpetuated through media representations of religion (Devon, Plymouth and Torbay, 2007). All the agreed syllabus examined in research for this book argue that RE is important because not only does it deal with ultimate questions and the purpose of life, but it cultivates the attitudes needed in a culturally diverse society. In the forward to the Bristol Agreed Syllabus, the Director of Education for the LEA, Heather Tomlinson, writes:

> ... successful and vibrant RE teaching is of foremost importance when embracing the culturally diverse needs in Bristol. To enable learners to develop local, national and global understanding and insights, they need access to a thoughtful and well informed RE curriculum.

How is it that RE came to situate itself as the curriculum area most closely associated with multiculturalism? The relationship between RE and the promotion of tolerance and mutual understanding has been recognised since *Learning for Living*, the key RE journal of its time 'ran a special edition in conjunction with the Commission for Racial Equality in the late 1960s' (Wright, 2007:111). The transformation of RE into a subject dedicated to the promotion of particular values is partly a legacy of earlier developments in RE, but it has happened in the context of key developments in education. The first was what was described as an attempt by the Christian right to re-establish the status and position of Christian education in RE and on the curriculum more generally (Copely, 2003). As we saw in the last chapter, RE had moved away from an approach that was either confessional or focused only on Christianity. As a result of intense lobbying, Section 8 of the 1988 Education Reform Act demanded that the RE curriculum be 'disproportionately and discriminatingly weighted towards the study of Christianity' (Grimmitt, 2010) regardless of the religious background of the child and his/her family. Bates describes this move as setting back the gains of the previous decades where Shap and other likeminded educationalists had struggled to separate RE from the confessional teaching of Christianity (Bates, 1996).

The impact was to reaffirm the status of Christianity and to ensure the privileging of Christianity over other world religions but it also initiated a period of confusion for many teachers. Although the move was interpreted as an attack on the newly won secular underpinning for RE, it was more a compromise than a victory for either side (Copley, 2003). Schools were legally obliged to privilege the teaching of Christianity, but many teachers had been trained and were wedded to the principles underlying the pedagogies behind a world religions and phenomenological approach to RE. Grimmitt argues that it also stratified the approach to RE: the obligation for teachers to parcel out a proportion of time for each religion (always with more time for Christianity) encouraged teachers to teach religions in discrete sections (Grimmitt, 2010).

Secondly, the attempt to re-establish the relationship between RE and Christian education was made during a period of intense national debate over the relationship between race and education. The impact of these discussions on the representation of Islam in education is considered in detail in the next chapter. But there was also an impact on RE generally. Jackson argues that the many different pedagogies of RE developed in response to the increasing diversity in society (Jackson, 2004). In his analysis, the increasingly plural backdrop to English society provides the context for particular responses of pedagogies to racial, ethnic and cultural difference. Some pedagogies, like that most closely associated with his work on interpretive learning, see plurality as a positive development and seek ways of helping teachers and pupils to engage with aspects of that plurality. Some pedagogies are defensive, some reciprocate and others seek to reassert the claims of their own religious traditions. Jackson's analysis offers the potential for a more politicised and social understanding of the relationship between religion and education, as discussed in the last chapter.

The relationship between multiculturalism and RE entered a new stage during the 1990s that was characterised by an identification between RE and multiculturalism. Multicultural education was never conceived as belonging to any one part of the curriculum but was to inform all aspects and areas of education (Kincheloe and Steinberg, 1997). Yet in the 1990s, RE in schools became synonymous with multicultural teaching. This is evident in the ubiquitous references to the contribution of RE to multicultural education in agreed syllabi across the country as well as in textbooks.

There is a great deal of research on RE but it has tended to focus on pedagogies and discussions of the rationale and nature of RE rather than what actually happens in classes and schools. Although this means we know very little about the strategies and practices used by teachers behind the closed door of the classroom, we know a great deal about the dominant philosophies and pedagogies of RE. It lies outside the National Curriculum, but during the 1990s it began to model itself on the curriculum's structures and benchmarks (Kay, 2007). So, like every other National Curriculum subject, RE began to use the language of skills and objectives, knowledge and understanding (Grimmitt, 2000). Whereas the previous period could be characterised by the belief that inter-religious understanding and tolerance was one of the desirable aims of RE, those qualities now became the justification for RE's place in the curriculum. This was an approach that suited the absence of any agreed core or coherent rationale for RE, but it also linked the fate of RE to the promotion of 'established values' throughout the curriculum.

That RE has come to play this role is not universally accepted as a positive development by RE specialists. Neither is there consensus about the aims and objectives of RE or even the way it is assessed and structured (Teece, 2011). The domination of multiculturalism in schools, however, meant that the place of RE was safe. Its identification with the promotion of positive attitudes towards diversity and its positioning as an area dedicated to the development of skills that would help pupils negotiate the demands of a multi-faith, multicultural society, helped secure a place for RE in an increasingly crowded timetable. However, all this changed as criticisms of multiculturalism gained momentum by the end of the twentieth century.

Multiculturalism and Islam

A frequent criticism of multicultural education in the 1990s was that it was superficial and perpetuated a shallow and one-dimensional view of cultures. Barry Troyna summed up the superficiality of multicultural education in the phrase: 'saris, samosas and steel pans' (Troyna, 1983). The tendency in RE to present knowledge about religions through discrete categories of special buildings or sacred texts fragmented it into a series of headings.

The tendency for teaching and learning in RE to be shallow and broad is observed in many Ofsted subject reports including the recent *Making Sense of Religion* (Ofsted, 2007) and *Transforming Religious Education* (2010). A generation of children were taught Islam through lessons focused on designing prayer mats, learning to write their names in Arabic script and drawing geometric patterns. Individual lessons on art and practices associated with Muslim cultures can engage pupils in creativity and knowledge drawn from the Muslim world. However, if this is all they learn about Islam, their understanding can only be superficial, and they will not acquire even a cursory knowledge of Islam.

Multiculturalism may simultaneously mean nothing and everything (Kincheloe and Steinberg, 1997), but patterns and common assumptions can be identified in its many forms. Kincheloe and Steinberg describe five different models of multiculturalism: liberal, conservative, pluralist, left essentialist and critical. While there are important distinctions among these about the role of culture and the strategies for managing difference, they share an assumption that the differences between racial, cultural and ethnic groups can somehow be positively negotiated and that education has a role in this process (Joppke, 2004). The other significant shared factor is that, although individual theorists seek to position particular interpretations of multiculturalism within different political or philosophical frameworks, they must all ultimately pursue strategies or challenge ideas embedded within existing educational frameworks. This means that the underlying ideology behind key areas of education, the National Curriculum or policies, significantly affect the way multiculturalism is manifested in classroom practice. Schools do not implement or develop multicultural strategies in the abstract; they must all be implemented and channelled through existing educational structures and norms. The impact of multiculturalism in schools will always be contextualised by the framework of existing legislation and guidelines.

As a document, the National Curriculum provides a rigid and comprehensive structure for the transmission of values and political norms. It does this through its construction of subjects and the relationship between inspections and the use of skills and attitudes to regulate the outcome of learning. The beginning and the end of the National Curriculum document provide an explicit set of values that teachers and schools are expected to promote. The statement of values at the end covers all aspects of life in England: 'The Self, Relationships, Society and the Environment'.

The National Curriculum makes a number of assumptions about diversity and multiculturalism in relation to individual subject areas and the curriculum as a whole. Pearce argues that it promotes and protects a 'narrow white, male and middle class view of culture' (Pearce, 2005). Individual subjects areas, like Citizenship Education and History, are more commonly perceived as enforcing an ethnically exclusive interpretation of events (Osler and Starkey, 2001). The comprehensive nature of the National Curriculum guidelines amounts to a description of a national character and ensures that any cultural practice or aspect of diversity that falls outside its parameters is automatically illegitimate. As a strategy, multiculturalism has always implied a core or base line of agreed values that constitute a boundary of agreed difference (Endres, 2002; Palumbo-Lu, 2002). For British education, those boundaries are clearly identified in the National Curriculum and other policies. A diversity of values and cultures is permitted and even celebrated but only as long as these fall within the values which are set out in bullet point form in the closing pages. Multicultural education survives as a classroom practice as long as the cultures it embraces do not challenge the established culture of the National Curriculum.

It was an awareness of Muslim communities as having a religious, ethnic and political identity that was construed as at odds with British values and culture that gave credence to Phillips' and Cameron's distancing and critiques of multiculturalism. Generations of Muslim families who had lived and worshipped in Britain since the 1950s could exist as a silent if not invisible group – until the Salman Rushdie affair.

Before that, the presence of Islam in the UK was subsumed under other identities: Asian, Pakistani, Bangladeshi or Indian (Allen, 2010). The development of a vocal and visible identity that was Asian and Muslim, and concerned to defend itself against criticism, cast the notion of a distinct Muslim culture into the public consciousness. What appeared to energise the anger of numerous commentators was not that Muslim communities shared particular traditions or values but that their traditions and values lay outside the accepted boundaries of multicultura-

31

lism. When Trevor Phillips told *The Times* (2004) 'Multiculturalism does not mean anybody can do anything they like in the name of their culture', his words were a coded condemnation of Islam.

By the beginning of the 1990s a Muslim voice in British life was evident. A combination of foreign and domestic events served to situate Islam as politically, socially and culturally at odds with Britishness for many commentators. The Salman Rushdie affair helped to establish Islam as a source of extremism and fundamentalism. Talal Asad describes the protests and rows around the publication of *The Satanic Verses* as so severe that they provoked a political crisis (Asad, 1990). Rushdie's *The Satanic Verses* was published in 1988. Partly inspired by the life of the Prophet Muhammad, the novel offended many Muslims. In 1989 Ayatollah Ruhollah Khomeini of Iran issued a fatwa against Rushdie.

The Rushdie affair alerted many in the UK to the presence of an articulate British Muslim voice and this placed Islam at the heart of a new debate about the limits of multiculturalism. Before Rushdie, 'being British and Muslim did not seem to clash. Fighting for Muslim rights did not seem to imply dual loyalties' (Werbner, 2005:16). In the media and public imagination, the fact that so many Muslims could be offended by a work of fiction showed the irrationality of Muslim sensibilities; it was an illustration of how far they were from the western liberal ability to recognise satire (Morey and Yaqin, 2011).

The conflict between Iran and Iraq, between Iraq and Britain and America, and the war in Afghanistan reinforced the idea that Muslim countries were prone to violence and followed practices perceived as illiberal. The attacks on the Twin Towers appeared as the culmination of two decades of increasingly fanatical Muslim rage. David Gillborn argues that 9/11 saw a marked change in the way that multiculturalism was perceived by the public and in political debates. Not only were politicians more likely to challenge previously accepted tenets of multiculturalism but there was a growing public mood of retribution and anger against Muslims that 'crystallised into an all-out attack on multiculturalism' (Gillborn, 2008).

There is a correlation between the development of a visible Muslim identity in the UK and the growing hostility to the presence of that identity in discussions about equality, discrimination in political life.

There is also a correlation between the rise of an awareness among the non-Muslim majority of a Muslim identity and a consensus that Muslim culture undermines multiculturalism. It is not clear, however, why this is so. After all, Muslim families are not the first or only communities to live in particular geographical areas. Other individuals, too, wear clothes that are recognisable as belonging to a certain group, and other communities have values and beliefs that could be interpreted as falling outside the remit of traditional liberalism.

Segregation along racial and ethnic boundaries is nothing new in Britain, and issues of inequality in education and employment have been and still are associated with certain groups (Tomlinson, 1983). Particular values and attitudes are commonly linked with Islam in education. Farid Panjwani argues that a common feature of the representation of Islam in the agreed syllabi and in resources for schools is that Islam is routinely perceived through an exclusively religious lens so that all practices, beliefs and traditions are interpreted in this light (Panjwani, 2005). A closer look at the arguments used to associate Islam with the limits of multiculturalism suggest that it is not just Islam that is being scrutinised, but also the values associated with Islam.

A familiar argument is that the practices and beliefs of Islam stretch the limits of western toleration too far. In 2006, former Foreign Secretary Jack Straw suggested that women who wear niqab may make relations between communities worse. He asked Muslim women who visited him wearing niqab to consider removing it. His remarks were interpreted as a statement that the difference chosen by Muslim women was problematic in a way that the differences chosen by, say, Sikh women was not. His objection to having to talk to one of his constituents while she was wearing niqab was rooted in the values he associated with that clothing.

Straw's comments can be interpreted as crass and Islamophobic but his focus on the nature of the difference represented by Muslims is a common theme in the debate about Islam and the limits of multiculturalism (Allen, 2010). Ibrahim Kalin argues that multiculturalism has reached its limits in the current debate over Muslims and Islam because it is framed, determined and premised by the 'secular-liberal ideals of the European Enlightenment, which cannot accommodate a non-Western religion such as Islam' (Kalin, 2011:5). Kalin believes that Western liberalism privileges secularism so that any notion of the subject that is not defined by the privatised, rational individual of modernity is either illegitimate or at best compromised. People or communities that choose to prioritise or accentuate a religious or spiritual identity can be viewed as challenging secular behaviour or values. Again this is an interpretation that is based on the idea that the difference in values between liberalism and Islam are fundamentally incompatible.

The other common critique of multiculturalism is that the celebration of difference leads to the legitimisation of segregation, and this theory also rests on the importance of values. In 2005, columnist Melanie Phillips wrote an article on the London 7/7 bombings headed 'This lethal moral madness' (Phillips, 2005).

'The moral madness' she refers to was the insistence by many Muslim leaders, including Sir Iqbal Sacranie, then general secretary of the Muslim Council of Britain, that Islam is a religion of peace. She identifies the 'cultural brainwashing' that she sees as part of a multicultural agenda that refuses to teach Muslims and other minorities 'the core of British culture and values' as the cause of a radical identity that rejects Britishness (M. Phillips, 2005). Phillips' condemnation of the pursuit of separateness rather than of a united British culture is echoed in Trevor Phillips' claim in 2005 that the nation is 'sleepwalking into segregation' and that we are polarised by faith and culture as never before (T. Phillips, 2005).

The association between Islam and the failure of multiculturalism was credible because many of the issues highlighted by its critics were already established as problematic. Serious social problems to do with housing, education, discrimination and unemployment were linked with the failures of multiculturalism (Tomlinson, 2008). However, the relationship between Islam and the limits of multiculturalism are important as this connection legitimates the adoption of assimilationist and integrationist approaches to ethnic and racial difference. Most models of multiculturalism are based on a recognition that difference is acceptable, even desirable and that pupils were encouraged to celebrate. The failures that are identified with multiculturalism – ethnic segregation, divided communities, inequalities in education and employment, the absence of shared values – are blamed on the communities that have failed to integrate.

Policies that champion assimilation and integration are based on the premise that this is a society with common beliefs, one in which communities should be willing to integrate or, as Prime Minister Blair said, have a 'duty to integrate' (Blair, 2006). In a context where multiculturalism is deemed to have reached its limits, it is the minority communities and Muslim communities in particular that are held responsible for existing on the margins of society. Discrimination, the failure to acknowledge difference and the lack of resources are no longer seen as factors in social segregation.

Integrationist views are evident in immigration policy and the treatment of refugees and asylum seekers. The Immigration, Asylum and Nationality Act of 2006 gives the state the power to remove British citizenship from individuals with dual citizenship if the Home Secretary believes this to be 'conducive to the public good' (Branigan, 2005). The drive towards integration is also apparent in education and especially the community cohesion agenda.

Nowhere is the relationship between the discrediting of multiculturalism and the rise of integration as the legitimate approach to issues of ethnicity and race more evident than in the *Cantle Report*. Ted Cantle chaired the Community Cohesion Review Team set up by the government in the wake of the riots in Bradford and other northern cities in 2001. His Home Office Report in 2001 and his 2008 book discussing the team's findings urged policies that stressed cohesion and integration in the context of the failings of multiculturalism. Much of the book is devoted to pointing up the inadequacies of multiculturalism for modern British society.

As a strategy for negotiating ethnicity and race, integrationism is inherently regulatory. Not only is the onus placed on groups to fit in but when assimilation is the benchmark, the commitment to integrate into a form of Britishness can be used to measure the degree to which communities integrate. Muslim groups that insist on making a commitment to Islamic practices and beliefs are, by definition, disengaging from integration. This is why Jack Straw objected so strongly to the niqab. It appears as though the values associated with niqab defy integration.

35

When politicians talk about the need to assimilate, they are not talking about common attitudes to food or music or other aspects of culture, they are talking about common values as located in the idea of British-ness. And it is the stress on core values, shared values or common values that singles out British Muslims as outsiders, because Islam is defined by values that are held to be alien to everything British. Aspects of Muslim dress, gender relations, Muslim schools, Muslim law, funda-mentalist Islam, Islamacism, the Islam of Al Qaida, are all understood to be not merely cultural differences but differences in values. As dis-cussed in the next chapter, the significance of Islamic values and the threat of Muslim radicalism is a dominant theme in every aspect of Home Office Strategy counter-terrorism strategy, from *Contest* and the school-based initiatives of *Prevent.*

The notion of maintaining difference is now widely seen as problematic. When David Cameron warned against multiculturalism in Munich, he was condemning groups that failed to promote 'British' values. Not only is difference held to lead to segregation, but difference represents a re-jection of Britishness.

The presence of Islam as a distinct, apparently cohesive and vibrant community with its own values was interpreted as an affront to British-ness. It seemed to bear out the decades of warnings from traditionalists that cultural segregation and the fragmentation of core values was a consequence of multiculturalism. The growing visibility of Islam as a religion and its associations with values which were perceived as testing the limits of British sensibilities, rendered multiculturalism incapable of negotiating diversity. Rejection of multiculturalism went hand in hand with the introduction of initiatives designed to restructure the relationship between communities and the state, particularly the com-munity cohesion agenda explored in Chapter Four. Tensions between multiculturalism as a strategy for teaching about difference, the public perception of Muslims as resistant to integration, and the consistent failure of education to deal with questions of ethnicity and inequality, all reverberated on the representation of Islam in schools.

3

Teaching and learning – the raw materials

Religious Education textbooks about Islam follow the formula for textbooks on other religions and aim to portray Muslims positively. I show that when we consider omissions and the failure to identify and contextualise Muslims in Britain however, Islam is portrayed in textbooks in a way that inhibits engagement with many of the issues that impact on Muslims. In most textbooks Muslim beliefs and practices are interpreted in a way that would be sympathetic to a Western audience and often omit controversial or political issues. This chapter argues that while some of these trends are evident in the representation of other religions in textbooks, the impact on the portrayal of Islam is more profound because of the place of Islam in narratives outside the classroom.

In 2010 the Board of Education for the state of Texas passed a resolution calling on all publishers to correct pro-Islamic/anti-Christian bias in textbooks for schools. The three day meeting was organised after parents and educationalists along with representatives of the American Textbook Council, an organisation that reviews history and social studies textbooks, argued that current world history books favour Islam. They claimed that current books provide sanitised definitions of Jihad, whitewash Muslim involvement in slavery and ignore Muslim practices involving sexism and the position of women.

Six months earlier, Muslim parents and the civil rights group, the Council on American Islamic Relations (CAIR) launched a campaign against a series of textbooks, *The World of Islam*, that they believed were promoting anti-Muslim attitudes amongst children. Moein Khawaja, the director of CAIR, called on schools and libraries to exchange *The World of Islam* for *Introducing Islam*, another series of books from the same publishing house, Moon Crest Publishers. Khawaja claims that the textbooks from The World of Islam series reinforce anti-Muslim feeling by claiming that Islam in Europe is the source of 'all social conflict' (Radu, 2009).

The two disputes, both focused on the representation of Islam, illustrate the polarised nature of debates about Islam in the curriculum. What one group believes is a textbook with a sympathetic portrayal of Islamic beliefs is characterised by others as a deliberate attempt by the authors to falsely represent Islam in a way that would make it more attractive to Westerners. In his review of textbooks used in American social studies lessons, Gilbert Sewell claims that there is a tendency to 'fuzz' the truth about aspects of Islam. He claims that in the commonly used *The Modern World*, published by Prentice Hall, the position of women in different Muslim countries is portrayed as varying from place to place. He argues that this is not entirely true and that, in failing to discuss how some women are subjected to 'housebound seclusion' and may be 'shunned, oppressed and punished', textbooks are blurring the facts and using 'language designed to circumvent harsh truths' (Sewell, 2008). Alternatively, Alex Luxenburg, author of *Radical Islam*, part of The World of Islam series, claims that his books are telling the truth about the effects of radicalised Islam although opponents have labelled them 'misleading' and full of 'inflammatory rhetoric' (*Reuters*, 17.3. 2010).

The American arguments over the presentation of Islam in textbooks are not surprising. Textbooks occupy a peculiar place in the classroom. As books that are specifically written and designed to educate, they are usually presented as neutral and objective sites of truth. It is accepted that books intended for adults may promote one version of history over another but books for children and especially books for use in school should be seen to be objective and fair. This is why all sides in the American debates about Islam in textbooks argue that they are for or against the use of certain books in school because of how they represent the truth.

Debates about textbooks may tell us how different groups perceive Islam but an examination of the textbooks themselves tells us more. All textbooks are the communication of a narrative, that is, an interpretation of events or beliefs that are carefully selected for the purpose of education. In the case of textbooks about Islam, they contain a particular type of narrative, what Jonker and Thobani call a 'pedagogic representation of Islam' (Jonker and Thobani, 2010:1). They argue that the presentation of knowledge, the selection process that decides whether one event should be prioritised over another, the style of telling, all constitute the creation of a pedagogic representation of Islam. Sewell analysed the representation of Islam in American social studies textbooks and he describes the technical challenge of trying to squeeze more than 1400 years of history, religious thinking and interactions with the rest of the world into lesson sized chunks (Sewell, 2008). But this is a naïve interpretation of the process; interpreting knowledge so that it is accessible and manageable for teachers and pupils is a factor but these challenges are considered within the context of a previously chosen narrative. Behind the design of every textbook are assumptions about why this subject is taught, how it should be taught and the nature of the subject itself.

Examining different textbooks allows us to see how those representations differ and identify common themes and assumptions – but this is true for all textbooks. In the case of Islam, especially in relation to the most recent period, textbooks take on a more significant role in education for several reasons. The first is that recent subject reports on Religious Education by Ofsted note that teachers of RE are often non-specialists with poor subject knowledge (Ofsted, 2007). Where teachers themselves lack confidence in a subject they are less able to spot inaccuracies or challenge prejudices in books.

Furthermore, in a climate where associations between Islam, terrorism, radicalism and threats to national security are widespread, the representation of Islam in textbooks takes on particular importance. Douglass and Dunn characterise textbooks as the embodiment of not just a narrative but officially sanctioned narratives (Douglass and Dunn, 2002). If this is the case it is important to understand how contemporary text-books are situated within these discourses. Do they reflect common Orientalist assumptions, do they mirror and perpetuate popular percep-tions of Islam or are they situated as part of some other narrative? Do textbooks written explicitly for use in the classroom mirror and per-petuate dominant narratives on Islam or are they representative of dis-courses located within education?

This chapter analyses recent trends in the way Islam is represented in textbooks for RE and Citizenship Education. Islam appears in other parts of the curriculum, most noticeably history, but the debates and issues that surround the representation of Islam in the history syllabus are so intertwined with debates about the role and nature of history itself that they cannot be properly unpacked here. The question at the heart of my analysis is how textbooks on Islam in RE and Citizenship Education have excluded discussions about Islam and the nature of representations of Islam in those subjects. Particular attention is paid to what is missing from many of the textbooks and the way presenting an abstracted and narrow view of Islam prevents any meaningful engage-ment with Muslim lives.

Textbooks and RE – the bigger picture

There are two recent significant research projects that have either focused on the use of textbooks in RE or looked at them as part of a larger project. Before looking at Islam in textbooks, it is worth consider-ing the findings of this research, not only because some of the issues to do with the representation of religion generally overlap but also be-cause they raise pertinent questions about the relationship of textbooks to the curriculum.

In 2010, the Department for Children, Schools and Families (DCSF) published an extensive report on the materials used to teach RE across all key stages. The *Materials used to Teach about World Religions in Schools in England* report was carried out by the Warwick Religions and Education Research Unit and is the most thorough overview in the UK in this area to date. The Warwick team analysed textbooks and also digital resources. They looked at the books themselves as well as how they were used and the factors that contributed to their use in the class-room. Significantly, they also focused on their contribution to education for community cohesion in relation to pupil learning about the principal religions and also on the messages implied about factors relating to inter-religious dialogue and cooperation between communities.

Yet another ongoing research project on RE at Glasgow University has included an examination of the nature and use of textbooks in education. *Does Religious Education Work?* is a large three-year investigation into the practices and outcomes of religious education funded by the ESRC. The approach of the project was to analyse and investigate RE from as many perspectives as possible. As part of this extensive project, the project team observed RE in 24 schools, interviewed students and teachers, reviewed policies, agreed syllabi and assessed a range of resources.

Both projects discovered a number of factors about the composition, development and use of textbooks in schools that contribute to a more comprehensive understanding of the way Islam is represented. The strength of both reports is that they were able to examine not just a single factor in the teaching of RE but to look at the teaching, the use of textbooks and the implied pedagogy in the context of the school as a whole. Their close observation of classroom practices alongside their data on the policies of schools and teacher attitudes allowed them to piece together a broad and detailed description of the environment in which textbooks are used. Both reports highlighted the personal commitment and creativity of many RE teachers, and noted that most textbooks and pedagogies were informed by a desire to cultivate a sense of the depth and significance of the contribution of religion to the modern world.

The DCSF research audited over one hundred textbooks across four key stages that are in use today. They found that a wide range of resources is used by teachers who regularly use textbooks as well as creating their own resources from other areas including the internet. They found that teachers are concerned to find materials that are creative, inspiring and appropriate for their pupils (DCSF, 2010). As part of the project, in-depth case studies were carried out in certain schools where teaching was observed, resources examined and teachers interviewed. They found that most teachers were committed to celebrating the role of

41

religion and that many chose textbooks precisely because they helped them to emphasise respect and tolerance for others.

Although the ESRC project is still on-going, the team have published their preliminary findings, indicating that teachers of religion are usually enthusiastic, committed to their subject and promote the contribution of religion to society throughout lessons (Lundie, 2010). Both projects made positive observations about the content and use of RE textbooks. They recognise that the majority of contemporary RE textbooks emphasise the contribution of religions to culture and morality and encourage pupils to respect the traditions, beliefs and practices associated with different religions.

Both reports, however, found that the usefulness of textbooks is compromised by inaccuracy and imbalance and that the text is often superficial. The DCSF report noted that although textbooks on Islam were often of a high quality and gave the impression that Islam was a living religion with a secure place in Britain, 'accounts of the religion were sometimes rather simplistic'. Muslim reviewers recommended using fewer textboxes and flow charts and giving more space to substantial explanations (DCFS, 2010:99).

Perhaps the most significant factor in the design of textbooks was the impact of examinations. The DCSF report noted that at Key Stage 4 'books related primarily to examination requirements' (DCSF, 2010:4). This meant that the books had a narrow focus, and that there was an imbalance between different types of learning in relation to RE and also that the nature of the issues covered was influenced by the requirements of examinations. The imposition of exam requirements on textbooks means that examinations rather than other factors structure the presentation of knowledge as well as determining what should be included.

The ESRC report drew similar conclusions about the detrimental impact of exams on textbooks. Their data drew a picture of a subject where a circle of external factors impinge on the quality of teaching, the resources chosen and the way they are used. They established a pattern where the pressure of examinations seems to dominate the classroom while RE is given little time on the curriculum timetable. Consequently textbooks designed to help schools achieve good GCSE results are popular with teachers. Books that are explicitly linked to particular exam syllabi, with their exam style activities, their 'tips for students' dominate the market for RE textbooks at Key Stage 4. The conclusions drawn by the research is withering:

> These textbooks now have as their central aim not the furthering of particular forms of religious understanding, but the provision of limited material to answer exam questions. Unashamedly these books are marketed as texts for passing exams. (Conroy, 2011:13)

The ESRC and DSCF projects did not focus on the teaching of Islam in RE or specifically on textbooks about Islam. The close relationship between textbooks, examination boards and teaching is the same for all the religions taught in RE: the same narrowing of focus, the same restricted engagement with contemporary expressions of belief and practice. To understand how Islam is represented in textbooks we need to examine books that focus specifically on Islam. Two recent investigations by Panjwani (2005 and 2012) and Otterbeck (2005) into textbooks on Islam reveal a pattern of misinformation and ideological assumptions.

The observations made by Panjwani and Otterbeck about the quality, accuracy and contribution of the texts to pupil learning are more critical in almost every respect than the ESRC and DSCF research. This may be because the research projects considered texts on Islam as part of their investigation of far broader themes which covered all the principal religions.

The number of texts examined by Panjwani and Otterbeck is very small, although both authors argue that the books they chose to examine are from reputable publishing houses and frequently used in schools. Both authors suggest that the representation of Islam in textbooks is problematic.

The two authors provide a typology of errors, or common features drawn from their reading of the textbooks on Islam. Otterbeck examined seven texts from Sweden from the theoretical standpoint that no text was neutral but represented an object 'that was a tool of power in a discursive struggle' (Otterbeck, 2005). This author lists the following features:

> general structures of texts
>
> minor errors

confusing structures and information omitted

tendentious choice of facts

the fixation on Islamism and the invisibility of other forms of Islam

Otterbeck's review showed that textbooks regularly misrepresented Islam and the lives of Muslims in a variety of ways. Books presented stereotypical images of Islam. It wasn't only that books contained errors (although they did) or that use of certain images and language inferred universal qualities and made inaccurate generalisations (although they did that as well). It was all of the above combined with a pattern of 'blind spots' and implication by omission. This is what Otterbeck calls the 'tendentious choice of facts', where writers select text and images that imply and insinuate an image of Islam and Muslims. For Otterbeck this is particularly true in the way texts 'established a dichotomy of 'we' and 'they'', through the consistent presentation of Muslim beliefs and practices in isolation from history and of the continual representation of Muslims as a group rather than individuals.

Panjwani's analysis of school text-books on Islam is equally devastating. His typology is broader in character than Otterbecks' although, like Otterbeck, his critique embraces not only the words and pictures that make up the text but the underlying pedagogy and implications of learning about Islam. Panjwani identifies the following areas as foci for the misrepresentation of Islam:

Monolithic versus Pluralistic Presentation

Literalist versus Symbolic Understandings

Historical/humanist versus Absolutist Approach

He argues that the textbooks on Islam repeatedly make assumptions about the lives and beliefs of Muslims that are informed by constant generalisations in the area of history, theology and culture. The Muslims that populate RE textbooks have no diversity; they are the same ahistorical, culturally homogenous and religiously monolithic Muslim repeated through the pages of books designed to educate pupils about Islam:

Muslims in this portrayal have no internal variations, all Muslims accept the same doctrines, perform the same rituals, all Muslim women wear hijab, all mosques have a dome and a minaret, all Islamic art forbids the depiction of human images, all Muslims believe that God revealed the Quran in actual Arabic words, that the Prophet physically ascends to heavens in his mi'raj and that there is a physical bodily resurrection after death. Furthermore, in this depiction Muslim rule in the past was universally benevolent, where people of other religions were always free to practice their religions, where learning from other cultures was universally admired and where there was ubiquitous prosperity. (Panjwani, 2010)

Panjwani's claim is that textbooks are effectively perpetuating a model of Islam that is only selectively true. Facts relating to Islam and lives of Muslims may be individually true but they are not collectively true; the Muslim world as it is portrayed in the textbooks examined by Panjwani does not exist outside the pages of these books or the lessons they are used to supplement. Like Otterbeck, Panjwani identifies a form of mis-representation that takes place not through deliberate inaccuracies but through what he calls the 'selective tradition approach'. Any curriculum is a selection of facts and outlooks and no education can escape the task of deciding what to discard and what to privilege. Panjwani is not criticising the process of selectivity, which he recognises as necessary, but rather the rationale and outcome of that selectivity. In the case of the Islam in the curriculum this is one that perceives Islam through the narrowest of eyes.

Although Ottobeck and Panjwani are both critical of the way Islam is represented in textbooks, there is an argument that Islam is not a special case in many of the examples they describe. Ottobeck acknow-ledges that failing to examine the representation of other religions in textbooks is a significant weakness in his own research because he is unable to answer the question of whether the weaknesses are related specifically to Islam or whether all religions in RE textbooks are subject to the same generalisations.

Textbooks and Islam

A thorough examination of RE textbooks that either focus on Islam or include Islam in the coverage of a number of religions reveals a compli-cated and often contradictory picture.

My review of textbooks encompassed a variety of approaches. It in-cluded a historical comparison to see if the way Islam is represented in textbooks has changed. It examined textbooks from the same period and often the same publishing house or series but which covered other religions, so that comparisons could be made. It also included textbooks used to teach Citizenship Education so I could compare how the same issue or similar areas were presented.

I reviewed 68 books published between 1968 and 2011, most of them specifically written as RE or Citizenship textbooks. Half the books are focused exclusively on Islam although it is books for younger pupils that tend to concentrate on one religion. The majority of books for older pupils are published and written in partnership with the major exam boards in the UK. The only exceptions to this pattern are books published by Muslim publishing houses and books published over twenty years ago.

There were two starting points to the review. The first was recognition of the insights provided by earlier research, partly with a view to finding out if those conclusions remained valid when a larger sample was used. The second was consideration of the issues raised in other discussions about the representation of Islam. Other examinations of Islam in textbooks or the curriculum have either started with Said's *Orientalism* or at least trodden in his footsteps at some point in their journey (Otterbeck, 2005) and my analysis is no exception.

I began by analysing the representation of Islam in relation to other areas: film, fiction, the news and popular culture. A central methodological assumption of my inquiry is that education is not isolated from the treatment of Muslims and representation of Islam in other areas of public life. Different authors interpret the way Islam is represented differently, or relate this process to a particular understanding of Islamophobia, but there is a broad consensus that the misrepresentation of Islam in numerous forums exists. Some locate the misrepresentation as part of Britain's identity as a foreign power, an outcome of a new imperialism (Cole, 2005); others see it as an essential part of Oriental trends working their way through British society as they have done for the last two hundred years (Allen, 2010). While there may be a wider recognition that Islam and Muslims are consistently vilified, patronised and represented in ways that are disparaging, few authors have yet considered how these attitudes may cross disciplines and fields of study to the extent that they have shaped children's and teachers' textbooks.

I had three general aims. The first was to see whether books designed for teaching in schools were an exception to the endemic misrepresentation of Islam in other arenas. The second was to understand how the themes of misrepresentation identified in other areas – film, news etc – were realised in texts written for children and young people and whether it would it be possible to identify examples of Islamophobia or Oriental themes in these books. The third was to consider the representation of Islam in textbooks in the context of discussions within RE about the representation of religion more generally.

A review of the books revealed several broad themes.

Books on Islam are like other books

The comparison of books that cover different religions gives the immediate impression of sameness: textbooks on Islam are just like textbooks on other religions. Publishing houses often produce books on religions as a set, each book dedicated to one religion or a particular religious theme: sacred texts, special places, special people etc. The layout of these books, the content of chapters, design, approaches to setting out information, quotes from texts and activities are often identical. This pervasive sameness is as common in Key Stage 2 as it is for books and examination texts at Key Stage 4.

The replication of structure, chapter headings (and often chapter content as well) across books that deal with religions does suggest that religions are dealt with equally. There may be a sense of *deja vu* whenever one opens certain RE textbooks but the treatment of religions is equitable. No religion is given a greater number of pages; there is no suggestion that one religion is truer or more significant than any other. This is underlined by the fact that the structure of books and the presentation of books as part of a set means that it is rare that religions are ever considered alongside each other.

The underlying premise of most contemporary RE textbooks appears to be that the information and activities they provide should promote a positive image of religions. All religions including Islam are presented as sources of cultural richness and depth, they have all affected the development of history and societies for the good, their sacred texts are all profound and the impact of religions on believers and community

47

members contributes to community development, strong family ties and a coherent sense of identity. In all the books examined, Islam and Muslims were mostly presented as positively as every other religion.

Books by Muslim authors or Islamic publishing houses

A critical analysis of the presentation of Islam in textbooks might assume that textbooks produced and written by Muslims would be more sympathetic and less prone to generalisations, theological or cultural assumptions and stereotypes. However there is an established tradition in the publication of RE textbooks for members of the religion in question to be the authors of the books or to act as consultants. The value of faith representation in all aspects of RE is evident in the earliest textbooks and is reflected in the structure of RE as a curriculum subject where the actual syllabi used in school are written by Agreed Syllabus Conferences, the interfaith/educational groups mandated by law to develop the syllabi for schools.

The most noticeable difference in books published by Muslim publishing houses is that they are often written explicitly to support the faith development of children. However contemporary books written for younger children are frequently indistinguishable in style from the books produced by mainstream educational publishers. *The Food We Eat* written by Farah Sardar and published by Islamic Foundation Books is a good example of the many beautiful texts designed to introduce young children to basic ideas in Islam. Books written for older pupils are more likely to be noticeably different from books published by the mainstream educational publishers.

The textbooks published by Islamic Foundation Books and the Muslim Educational Trust are more detailed about Muslim theology and history and they have noticeably more detailed text. In their writing style and use of images they bear a resemblance to textbooks published twenty years earlier than their secular counterparts. They have an old fashioned feel about them, tending to transmit text in large blocs, and they are often less polished.

The substantial difference between these books and books published by the mainstream publishers, however, is that they are detailed, substantial and very thorough in their coverage of subject knowledge. In a comparison between the two types of textbooks, those published by the

Muslim publishing houses could be used to study for exams in a higher key stage, at A level rather than GCSE.

As noted by ESRC and the DCSF research, the close relationship between exam syllabi and book publishers has resulted in books that are written specifically for exams. For Islam and for other religions as well (apart from Christianity), it is almost impossible to find books suitable for Key Stage 4 pupils which cover subjects not structured by the demands of an OCR, AQA or EDExcel syllabus. One consequence is that while some issues that relate to the specific cultural and political place of Islam in society are considered, they are done so only as they relate to existing curriculum structures. The rigid regulation of subjects induced by the need to fit texts around exam requirements leaves no room for exploration of concerns that are specific to Islam or any other religion. A teacher wanting to teach 14 or 15 year olds about Islam but not wishing to use books that were written with a GCSE syllabus in mind could be advised to use books published by the Islamic publishing houses.

Then and now

Textbooks for schools age quickly, especially in their format and design. Contemporary books for RE are characterised by glossy covers, beautifully produced images and pages packed with different fonts, shaded boxes, activities, speech bubbles and bullet points. Books on Islam (or other religions) are no longer endless pages of densely packed text broken up by the occasional line drawing or grainy black and white photograph. However, the most obvious difference between textbooks published before 1990 and today is not the standard of publication but that the last twenty years has seen a huge homogeneity in textbooks, especially for older pupils. Older textbooks may not be as glossy as their modern counterparts but they have greater variety in style and approach. The books written as part of the Westhill project, last published in 1988, stand apart from almost every range of textbooks of the modern period because their approach, style and content is so different from books published since.

A review of textbooks on Islam published in the last forty years shows that there is great continuity in some areas and huge changes in both the content and the way issues and subjects are presented.

Almost every textbook that covers Islam generally rather than a specific aspect (the Quran, festivals) is structured in an almost identical fashion. Chapters cover the same material and emphasise the same facts. How consistently this is done becomes even more apparent in the way all the books present the history and origin of Islam. Most Key Stage 2 and 3 books have a section or chapter that covers the history of Islam, its origins in the Arabian peninsula, the revelation of the Quran and the life of Muhammad. In almost every book this narrative is presented in a style and tone that is repeated from book to book. Similarly, most books have a section or chapter on the Five Pillars of Islam and again the repetition in interpretation and style is clear.

While continuity is the most obvious characteristic for certain sections of textbooks, other areas, most noticeably sections dealing with women and the family, immigration and ethnicity and Islam in other countries, have changed dramatically. Ethnicity and immigration in textbooks is discussed later in the chapter but it is interesting to contrast the different approaches towards women in textbooks over a 25 year period.

Women and the family

In textbooks published between 1978 and 1988, the status and position of women – their relationship to the family, arranged marriages and dress – are explicitly acknowledged as being different from that of white English women. The customs associated with arranged marriages and often of marriage generally are often described as coming from another society. Wearing niqab or a veil is frequently given a religious as well as a cultural explanation and there are many references to the expectation that, as Muslim communities integrate into English society, Muslim women will be more likely to dress like English females. *Islam,* published in 1983 by Hulton, describes the wearing of the veil in Arab countries as an 'old' custom. It goes on to explain that in many countries the veil 'has almost disappeared'. The implication is that wearing the veil is not synonymous with the habits of modern non-Arab societies and that as Muslim women become more modern so their dress will alter accordingly.

Discussions in older textbooks about the status and dress of women in Muslim countries are more likely to make a connection between the undeveloped nature of these societies and the use of the veil or niqab.

Niqab is described in some books as part of the denial of women's rights and an expression of their lack of equality, while others state that the process of modernisation in these countries may bring about a situation where Muslim women are freer and more equal. Some books explicitly draw a parallel between the civilising impact of democracy and western values brought about by greater contact with Western countries and the possibility of greater equality for women.

Spotlight on Islam written by Valerie Quinlivan in 1984 is a good example of this. The author stresses that Islam revolutionised the position of women and gave them more rights than they had ever had. She explains that although women have rights, men have many rights over women and that many Muslim women will be forced to 'take decisions about how they want to live' as 'Western customs, books and films find their way into Muslim countries'. She comments that, as Muslim religious leaders clamp down, some 'girls [will] find they are less free to study and work in some areas' (Quinlivan, 1984). While there is an emphasis on explaining why women dress modestly, the explanations sometimes suggest that the position of women in Islam is a subservient one and that this subjugation is reflected in their dress. Not all books of this period approach the subject of women and dress in this way but the idea that there is a conflict between the West and the traditional status of women is a common theme in these books.

Contemporary textbooks explain different types of dress for Muslims and the status of women but the most obvious difference is the way this subject is covered. The use of the veil or niqab is normally described as part of religious observance and the requirement to dress modestly for both sexes is located in the Quran. Textbooks frequently draw a link between the amount of a Muslim woman's body that is covered and the degree of her faith; the implication is that the more devout a Muslim woman is, the more likely she is to wear niqab.

Contemporary textbooks describe women's dress but never pass judgement on the wearing of the veil. They describe Muslim traditions in relation to dress in the same tone as they describe differences in mosque architecture.

Unlike their counterparts of twenty years ago, most modern books are reluctant to pass judgement in other areas as well. When covered in

51

books for Key Stages 3 and 4, arranged marriages and polygamy are described neutrally. In *Islam in Today's World,* the authors make a link between arranged marriages and the types of decisions used to choose a partner in Western societies such as going to a dating agency or placing an advert in a magazine. There is an attempt to present arranged marriages as a matter of individual choice. The implication is that having an arranged marriage could be a choice that anyone might make regardless of ethnicity or religion (Lynch, Clinton and Orchard, 2005).

Another contemporary book, *Islam (OCR GCSE),* presents arranged marriage as a process whereby partners are chosen according to their qualities. In one activity, the Halal dating game, pupils can choose cards and complete an exercise that simulates the choosing of partners. In this particular context, not only are arranged marriages presented neutrally but the authors appear to present them as normal practice in Britain (Hassan, 2009).

The assumption that arranged marriages are merely cultural variations on marriage customs found anywhere in the world is reinforced by the advice provided in some books encouraging teachers to describe them objectively to pupils. In *Islam: Teacher's Resource Book* written to support teachers, the authors promote an approach that assumes any interpretation by the teacher would be misplaced, urging teachers to: 'Explain these customs in a sensitive way, avoiding making any value judgements about differences in customs and cultures' (Le Pla, 1996).

Citizenship Education textbooks and Islam

As curriculum subjects, RE and Citizenship Education share important aims. Both are committed to promoting tolerance between religious and ethnic groups; both aim to support pupil engagement with ideas they believe will foster greater communication and empathy between groups. They are both committed to presenting the contribution of religious and ethnic groups to society as positive and to provide images and text that show how different cultural groups are an integral part of British society.

The differences between the ways Citizenship books cover Islam can partly be explained by differences in the content of the curriculum. While religions are the focus for RE, they are one topic among many for

Citizenship, so religions have less coverage. However, many Key Stage 3 and 4 textbooks include religion as part of their portrayal of work on diversity and the tolerance of national and ethnic identities. So although Citizenship books are keen to promote positive messages about religion, they do so in a context that assumes the diversity of communities in the UK and also that religious and ethnic differences are political and social issues that pupils will have different views on. This assumption is reflected in the fact that religions are often discussed in the context of the role of the media. Consequently representation and the possibility of misrepresentation is an integral part of Citizenship's engagement with religions.

Omission as misrepresentation

This chapter began with the question of what textbooks could tell us about the way Islam is represented in schools. Textbooks are only one of many resources used by teachers and the most comprehensive textbooks cannot compensate for weak teaching, poorly trained teachers or schools that are unsympathetic to the teaching of religion. There is also evidence that many teachers create their own resources so that the poor quality of textbooks is not a significant factor in their teaching. *The Materials used to teach about world religions in schools in England* report found that teachers frequently used a wide variety of sources to plan their lessons (DCSF, 2010).

Yet textbooks are an important gauge and mirror of the ways in which society sees a subject. The images chosen for a textbook say something about the way society wants pupils to see that religion. Textbooks that focus on some issues and ignore others, or books that feature certain types of activities rather than others, are all sending signals about the way we want that religion to be seen and discussed within education.

The signals given out by contemporary textbooks on Islam are sometimes clear and obvious whereas some are subtle and complex. Modern books are all committed to presenting Islam as a vibrant religion that has made an astounding cultural and spiritual contribution to humankind's history and to the lives of millions of followers today. Some of the books are almost like glossy travelogues full of pictures of stunning mosques and exotic architecture and art, exquisite calligraphy and beautifully photographed Muslims in different types of dress.

There was almost no evidence of views that interpreted Islam as a religion that was inferior to other religions in any way. There were some errors but errors are not confined to books on Islam. The common structures used by many publishers to format the knowledge and activities in books contributes to the appearance of equality between the treatment of different religions but there is no doubt that for most of the authors of these textbooks, Islam is a religion of depth and richness that is an essential part of a global society.

Islamophobia, defined by the Runnymede Trust as a portrayal of Islam as inferior or inherently critical of the West (Runnymede Trust, 1997), was not an obvious feature of any contemporary textbooks examined. A more common tendency was the overt attempt to dispel some key myths and misconceptions about Islam and Muslims. Books for older pupils frequently address some misconceptions they might be expected to have about Islam. Where contemporary textbooks discuss marriage, they tend to acknowledge that readers might not distinguish between an arranged marriage and a forced marriage and take care to explain the differences and to stress that compulsion is forbidden in Islam. Similarly, some Key Stage 3 or 4 books recognise that readers might assume that Jihad refers to militant or violent action and take care to explain the variety of interpretations within Islam.

The positive and sympathetic tone of textbooks on Islam belies the nature and form of the representation of Islam. The idea of misrepresentation suggests that authors are deliberately or unconsciously presenting images and facts about Islam that are designed to besmirch or belittle Islam. However, as Douglass and Dunn (2002) point out in their survey of Islam in American textbooks, good will on the part of publishers, authors and teachers is not enough. Some critics argue that the curriculum as it currently exists does not serve the needs of Muslim children in community schools and that the degree of oversimplification and the narrowness of the approach distorts Islam to the extent that it is nearly impossible for pupils to gain a comprehensive understanding of it (Alibhai-Brown, 2001). These claims may be true but they are also true of every other religion taught in RE.

Misrepresentation can take different forms and one debate that has recently come to the fore is the misrepresentation that occurs through the imposition of a liberal hegemony in all areas of education. This analysis of the relationship between education, liberal values and religion is relevant because it contributes a better understanding of the different factors that affect the representation of Islam in textbooks. One criticism of the way religions in RE are presented is that religions in education are misrepresented to suit a particular ideological or policy agenda. There are a number of key thinkers in the field of RE, including Andrew Wright, Trevor Cooling, Philip Barnes and the late Terence Copley, who have problematised what can generally be called the domination of liberal values and assumptions in the field of education. Although there are significant differences between these writers, they have in common an objection to the interpretation of liberal values as normative. Andrew Wright argues that liberal values and notions of truth have come to dominate RE so that truth itself becomes conditional and relativised (Wright, 2007). Philip Barnes describes a process 'that runs like a thread through much of the post-confessional history' of RE, where a liberal paradigm means that each religion is as valid as every other (Barnes, 2007). The misrepresentation of religion is then located in the desire to elevate a sameness amongst different religious traditions and perceived truth.

The liberal impulse acts on all religions but in the context of Islam the process has particular consequences. Otterbeck (2005) and Panjwani both argue that misrepresentation takes place through a variety of mechanisms. Panjawani (2010) argues that the selectivity characteristic of textbooks on Islam serves to create an Islam that is idealised and repackaged in a form that is acceptable to liberal western sentiments.

Wright (2004) and Barnes (2007) argue that the trends identified by Otterbeck and Panjwani in their respective analysis of Islam in textbooks are an expression of a more general phenomenon in textbooks. They believe that the conceptualisation of RE as an engine for the promotion of liberal values and norms means that textbooks leave out those practices and interpretations that do not fit the image of religion they want to present. This process impacts on all religions including Christianity. Barnes argues that mainstream Christianity is legitimised through the exclusion from textbooks of denominations and styles of Christian worship, especially the growth of Pentecostalism (2007). The desire to promote only the good about religion, as defined by liberal markers, is a theme that acts like the red pen of the censor in textbooks. This is a process that shapes the writing and design of all books but it has a particular significance for textbooks on Islam.

The reshaping of religions to better serve a liberal agenda has a greater and different impact on the representation of Islam for a number of reasons. First, Islam is popularly conceived as the antithesis of liberal values. The representation of other religions may be equally false, misleading or subject to generalisation and distortion but they are popularly conceived as belonging to the group of religions that are spiritually rich and where the promotion of peace is the norm. Christianity is normally assumed to be the *de facto* religion of Western culture with Judaism its precursor, and Hinduism, Buddhism and Sikhism their exotic counterparts elsewhere. All these representations are false. All of them are a remoulding of history and beliefs but theirs is a misrepresentation that concurs with public opinion. Of all the world religions, only Islam is perceived as intrinsically anti-democratic, innately authoritarian and prone to the repression and subjugation of women, so that the portrayal of Islam as a religion that can be conceptualised within a liberal framework appears contrived, even if it is not.

The social and political environment in which Islam exists is another reason why the representation of Islam to fit liberal sensibilities has a greater impact. On a global level, Islam bears the burden of being the focus of numerous international conflicts as well as the locus of a perceived international network of terror, extremism and violence. On a domestic level, the fear is of Islam as a source of the unchecked flow of immigrants. These multiple contexts and associations spanning every level and facet of public life means that for Islam to be represented through a liberal prism, the lens must misrepresent the context in which Islam exists.

A significant difference between contemporary textbooks and those written thirty years ago is the way in which the discussion and presentation of Islam is positioned in relation to immigration and ethnicity. *A Muslim family in Britain* by Stephen Harrison and David Shepherd, published in 1980, and *Understanding Your Muslim Neighbour* by Muhammad and Maryam Iqbal, published in 1976 are typical examples of RE textbooks of that period. Both texts include the usual information on the Five Pillars of Islam, the life of Muhammad, the role of the Mosque and the Quran. The knowledge contained in these sections is almost identical to that provided in textbooks written nearly thirty years later.

What makes these books typical of the period, however, is that both situate their discussion of Islam within the contemporary status of Muslims in Britain; there is an explicit recognition that Muslims in the UK at the time are most likely to be first or second generation immigrants from ex-commonwealth countries. Both books adopt the form of following the journey or experiences of two Muslim children as they travel to England as immigrants or acclimatise and settle into English life and culture. Their stories recognise that the culture and traditions of their families are very different; that though they are legally in England, they are foreigners, they are Asian, 'settlers in a strange land' (Iqbal and Iqbal, 1976).

Both books normalise the experience of immigration, presenting it as something ordinary and rational. The many reasons for migration and for choosing Britain as a new home are carefully explained. Racism as a factor in the lives of Muslims is not explicitly addressed but many of the prejudices against immigrants are explored; why do many immigrants live in the same areas? Why do they dress and eat differently? Are they contributing to the economy or are they a drain on resources? Such questions are explicitly discussed and explained as misunderstandings or misconceptions. In each book the text is laid out as though it were holding an imaginary conversation with the reader and each misconception is considered in turn.

If one were reading just the text of a contemporary book on Islam without seeing the images one would never guess that the majority of Muslims in the UK are from Pakistan, Bangladeshi and the Indian subcontinent. The ethnicity of British Muslims is often invisible in the text, ignored as a descriptive factor in the representation of Muslims. The experience of Muslims as part of an ethnic minority group is omitted. The assumption is that to be a Muslim in the UK is the same as membership of any other group. The only differences between Muslims, Buddhists, or Christians and those who belong to secular organisations are in the buildings they visit and beliefs they hold. Some textbooks acknowledge the immigrant heritage of many Muslim communities but it is rare for this to be discussed. Even where it is mentioned, there is no reference to Islamophobia, racism, discrimination or even the fact that some Muslims speak a language or languages other than English or have family and friends who are recent immigrants to the UK.

Teachers wishing to move beyond a description and discussion of the religious beliefs and practices of British Muslims and examine the social and cultural context in which many live their faith could make use of Citizenship textbooks. At Key Stage 4, these are not unlike RE books: their structure, too, is dictated not by pedagogy but by the requirements of possible future examinations. The same chapter headings and the same emphasis on developing skills are repeated in book after book. However, because Citizenship education focuses on the public and political aspects of issues, pupils are often introduced to religion through a range of subjects scarcely considered in RE, especially at Key Stage 4, such as identity, community, difference, diversity, prejudice, the media, discrimination and racism. Islam is rarely considered as the focus of these topics but pupils are frequently asked to consider the role of the media in portraying different groups.

It is not just the difference in area and scope of subjects that allows Citizenship textbooks to introduce pupils to the environment in which Muslims live; the tone and assumptions underpinning the text in these books are often very different from RE textbooks. Although they are relentlessly positive about the nature and contribution of religion to society, Citizenship books are more likely to include discussion points that question some religious claims and contributions. While the over-all approach to religion in the UK is still positive, there is a more critical tone to some aspects. In the *GCSE Citizenship Studies* book for AQA, for example, Islam is not covered in any detail but is included under the remit of religions, while there are opportunities for pupils to look at a range of controversial issues regarding identity and stereotypes which do not assume that religion is always positive (Campbell and Patrick, 2010). This is not to say that Citizenship textbooks or even the Citizen-ship curriculum are without their critics about how they promote identity. Audrey Osler and Hugh Starkey have frequently challenged the closed and exclusive nature of identity as it is expressed in Citizenship

Education and assert that the curriculum perpetuates a narrow view of identity and community (Osler and Starkey, 2001).

Teachers whose use of textbooks is limited to RE texts, however, will find that in relation to Islam the overwhelming impression is of ethnic blindness. In not elevating or even including the issue of Islamophobia or acknowledging the ethnicity of the majority of Muslims in this country, authors might be hoping not to make race or discrimination an issue. If their aim is to cultivate a sense and appreciation of the spiritual depth and complexity of Islamic religious beliefs, they may want to avoid making associations between conflict, disadvantage and Islam. In their aim to present Islam as a religion that is equal in every respect to all others, they focus on common experiences rather than identifying the specific challenges faced by followers of this religion.

RE textbooks that omit Islamophobia or issues of race and immigration from their representation of Islam are presenting Islam in a cultural and political vacuum. The vacuum is invisible in textbooks because other religions are presented in the same sanitised fashion, but it is the omissions of the experiences of Muslims in the UK and the significance of Islam domestically and internationally that are so glaring. Panjwani (2010) maintains that a key weakness of the way Islam is represented in textbooks is that it is always presented as a religion rather than as a culture, civilisation or source of identity. However, the tendency to isolate religious practices and beliefs from the social life of a community inevitably leads to a focus on abstract principles, historical events or doctrinal truths. The presentation of Islam as a pristine religious tradition is all that is left once every shred of political or cultural context has been removed.

Because of this liberal perspective there is a dual and seemingly contradictory process of representation and misrepresentation of Islam. The textbooks all say one thing, but the media tell other stories. Islam is considered in relation to education, urban regeneration, community cohesion, national identity and international relations. The image shown by policy makers or the media differs according to which aspect of Islam is highlighted or ignored. There are particular themes associated with Orientalism and the Other that are repeated, adapted and regenerated with each round of state intervention into immigration policy, race relations and international relations. These interpretations of Islam, themselves the product of myriad other forces, shape and inform public discussion.

The intensely politicised Islam of community cohesion, the Islam that subjugates women, the Islam of extremism and terrorism are all part of the public and popular images of Islam that are perpetuated through the media, and public and policy discussions on inequality and terror. However these Islams are not evident in textbooks – the image of Islam is transformed at the doors of the classroom from a religion/civilisation/way of life shaped by values, practices and beliefs to a religion comparable to other religions in every way.

The dual nature of the representation of Islam means that the image that is created in the public domain is then reframed to fit the liberal agenda required by education. The peaceful Islam where the Quran is a source of values and spirituality for millions all over the world, where equality and justice are intrinsic parts of key religious beliefs and festivals, is perpetuated through textbooks, exams, agreed syllabi and the curriculum in apparent contradiction to the Islam portrayed outside the school gates.

The full extent of this dual representation is clearly illustrated if we focus on the way gender issues and equality are represented in textbooks.

Women, Islam and textbooks

The discussion of the representation of Islam in policy and the media usually identifies the position of women as a salient factor in that representation and a clear picture of how women and gender issues are understood in the public gaze supports an understanding of the dual nature of representation found in textbooks. The status of women in Islam is at once the most visible expression of Islam and its most symbolic opposition to Western values and civilisation. People who know nothing of Islam believe that a woman wearing a veil is subjugated and oppressed; even if they know so little that they do not know she is a Muslim. The nameless Muslim woman who wears hijab or niqab perfectly embodies the antithesis of freedom, liberty and equality (sexual and every other kind). Her invisible body and face are an affront to modern people who believe her hidden body represents the secrecy and authoritarianism at the heart of Islam as well as a refusal to embrace the norms and values of a modern, forward, thinking society. The stereotype of the mute Muslim woman is representative of Muslim women everywhere so that, even if she is unveiled and vocal, it is perceived that she is only so because she is breaking free from Islam (Khan, 2002).

Media coverage of Muslim women is a genre in its own right, be it in the press, documentaries and the numerous novels and biographies that recount the struggle of Muslim women to escape Islam. It opines on the inequalities inherent in Muslim dress, arranged marriages, child brides, the treatment of women under sharia law, and the politics of the body. In April 2011, the French government banned the wearing of the burqa and niqab in public, demonstrating the extent to which they regarded Islamic dress as an affront to French values and democracy. Two hours after the ban took place, two women wearing burqas were arrested outside Notre Dame Cathedral. Politicians across the spectrum of French politics united to support the ban. Although the French reaction to a handful of Muslim women choosing to wear a certain style of clothing is extreme, it is in tune with the way British and other Western commentators have discussed women and Islam.

The associations of repression and inequality are so intimately tied to Islamic dress codes that even a hint of acceptance can provoke a barrage of media interrogation. When Nigella Lawson, a woman who has celebrated her voluptuous body as part of her career, appeared in a burkini on an Australian beach in 2011, she provoked an immediate debate about why 'an icon of sexy English femininity' is 'choosing to don sharia-compliant clothing' (Bunting, 2011). Lawson's wearing of the burkini, a bathing costume that fully covers the body, which she bought from a Muslim swimwear website, provoked an intensity of feeling that managed to inspire as many column inches as any news item that week. Amidst the discussions about Lawson's motives was the debate about the freedom of women to dress as they please and how far these freedoms should be accommodated in a free society.

The premise that Islam oppresses women through clothing or that Islamic law and religious practices are innately oppressive to women is a long-standing theme in the representation of Muslim women.

Although the French Government's response to women who wear niqab was severe and the response of the British press to one celebrity chef choosing to cover her body on a beach was ridiculous, both reactions perfectly captured the confusion and even rage generated over how Muslim women should look.

The extensive literature on Orientalism and Islam as the symbolic Other consistently identifies gender and its portrayal as a key Orientalist theme. The veiled Muslim woman is the antithesis of the Western woman who is free, liberated, allowed to express her sexuality and is equal to the men in her society. The presumed violence against the free will of Muslim women is suggestive of the violence of terrorism. Theresa Saliba describes a New York photo essay where the image of a veiled woman is juxtaposed with the photos of the Twin Towers (Saliba, 2002). The image of the veiled woman is so eloquent that sometimes it needs no text at all. In his research on the visual representation of Muslim and Arab women in US newspapers, Ghazi-Walid Falah found that the pictures of Muslim women rarely relate directly to the subject matter of the text, suggesting that the images serve some other purpose (Falah, 2005).

This pervasive and entrenched representation of Muslim women is only about how some of them dress. Saliba (2002) points out that all the assumptions make broad generalisations, but that there is no such thing as a typical Muslim woman. Muslim women are from different countries, classes, ethnicities and generations. The assumption that Muslim women wear particular clothing is not always symbolic of religious, cultural or gendered meaning. Sometimes women wear hijab because of family or peer pressure, or because they want to fit in, or because they want to make a point about their religion; some have feminist justifications. In *Does My Head Look Big in This?* Randa Abdel-Fattah gives a fictionalised account of a young woman who, after watching an episode of the sitcom *Friends* while on the running machine at the gym, decides that she will wear the hijab. She describes her feelings of anxiety (years of being taunted as a nappy head have given her an inkling of some of the abuse she can expect to receive) but also her feelings of release and of 'coming home' (Abdel-Fattah, 2006).

The representation of women that is persuasive in the media is absent from textbooks. You would never know from textbooks the assumptions about the status of women in Islam or the degree of hostility that exists in the West towards women wearing a veil. The multiple and complex reasons that prompt some Muslim women to dress in a particular way are sometimes addressed in books for young people but the emphasis is usually on religious and theological explanations that are divorced from all social, political and cultural contexts. Textbooks tend to present a woman's dress in Islam as a matter of choice.

In one GCSE textbook on Islam a picture of an unveiled woman in her marriage gown, her bodice diaphanous, is set opposite a dramatic picture of the face of a woman fully veiled. The text explains that the choice of dress is very complex for some and says that some women in Muslim countries wear 'traditional garb, using it as a symbol to disassociate themselves from what they see as a corrupting Western influence' (Green and Mayled, 2009). What is missing is any discussion of the relationship between women's dress and issues of equality. While textbooks can't cover every aspect of every issue, wider cultural or political factors are usually absent from RE textbooks.

The Ofsted report *Making Sense of Religion* noted that although religion's impact on society was significant, RE largely ignored controversies and the study of religion. The criticism made by Ofsted that RE often fails to address the social context in which people are religious and that this limits pupil understanding and enjoyment (Ofsted, 2007) applies also to gender and Islam. Issues that relate to gender are normally presented in a context that is simple and without nuance. Theological explanations of gender and other issues in textbooks are not juxtaposed with explanations that provide a cultural or political view.

By providing only the narrowest lens through which pupils can view any aspect of Islam, textbooks nurture certain prejudices and assumptions. They may seek to present a positive view of Islam and to encourage pupils to respect other cultures but they do so at the cost of casting light on Islam as it exists and is experienced.

The inadequate representation of Islam in textbooks is not due to one single factor. It ranges beyond RE or even Islam. Questions arise about the relationship between exams, textbooks and the syllabus in education more generally. Islamophobia and Orientalist themes influence the portrayal of Islam and the lives of Muslims but are mediated through modern preoccupations and relationships. Stereotypes and prejudices that originate in colonial relationships between the West and the Other are perpetuated and re-formed by current domestic politics and contemporary international relations and reappear in modern textbooks (Jonker and Thobani, 2010). However, Islam is mostly taught through RE, and consequently the dialogues and pedagogies that dominate RE intertwine with longstanding Orientalist ideas.

The reframing of Islam so that it adheres to liberal values is especially significant for Islam precisely because in popular discourses it does offend liberal sensitivities. So teachers are obliged to use books that promote a version of Islam that is sanitised and which offer few opportunities to engage pupils in debates that can challenge Islamophobia or clarify misconceptions. There is little research on teachers and Islamophobia but studies on teachers' understanding of racism and discrimination suggest that they are unlikely to be unequipped to deal with the gap between the awareness of Islam pupils have acquired from the media and the Islam of RE textbooks. Textbooks on Islam present a view of Muslim beliefs and communities that appears to be positive – but in a context that is divorced from the world in which pupils encounter Islam through other channels. Inaccuracies and prejudices are unacceptable in any book but the most significant aspect of representation in textbooks on Islam is what is not there, what is missing and what is not addressed.

4

Islam, education and
the Home Office

In November 2007, in a statement to the House of Commons, the Prime Minister affirmed the importance of religious education and the teaching of world religions. This was in a speech on neither education nor even community cohesion but on national security. In January the following year I made a quip at the QCA/NASACRE conference saying that, for the first time, RE had become a form of counter-terrorism. I would not make that same quip now, nor would an audience laugh, because that is precisely where RE now finds itself in the national Prevent agenda. (Miller, 2010)

The Home Office sees the teaching of Islam and other world religions as a key part of their strategy to oppose terrorism. The beginning of the new millennium was characterised by the explicit recognition in policies for schools and local authorities that Muslim communities represented a potential threat to national security. The threat was physical, taking the form of rioting, urban disturbances and acts of terrorism. But the perceived unwillingness of Muslim communities to integrate and their perceived failure to adopt customs and values that were not western was also seen as threatening. In response, first the Labour and then the Coalition Government introduced guidelines that explicitly confronted these issues and identified the need to monitor and regulate Islam and Muslim communities.

The community cohesion initiatives introduced in 2002 and thereafter, the *Prevent* strategy introduced in 2007 and again in 2011 by the Home Office, the requirement announced in 2008 for schools to write and adopt community cohesion strategies and the introduction of a school-based mentoring programme, REsilience, to halt the spread of extremism are all measures that implicitly identify Islam as a threat to society.

This chapter explores the ways in which Islam is repeatedly represented through policies that relate to education as a community or religious ideology that is associated with radicalism. The strategies mentioned above are discussed and the chapter argues how they combine to create a circular dialogue that contextualises every discussion of Islam. The chapter considers the key initiatives designed to manage the perceived threats associated with Islamic radicalisation and its links with education. Finally, it considers the nature of the relationship between RE as a community of practice and other government initiatives.

In particular, the chapter examines the way the state plays an increasingly explicit role in both the framing of debates about Islam, extremism and education and how particular approaches legitimise assumptions about the nature of Islam, Muslim communities and the place of shared values in society. Arun Kundnani (2007) and Shiraz Thobani (2010) both identify the role of the state as key to the creation of factors that promote Islamophobia and stereotypes of Islam throughout society. I argue that materials intended for schools, including those produced by REsilience, do not challenge those prejudices because they never refute the core of racism and hostility against Muslims. These materials do seek to present Islam and Muslim communities positively – but encouraging teachers and pupils to consider Islam sympathetically without engaging with the argument that Islam is illiberal leaves existing prejudices and assumptions unchallenged.

Community cohesion

Of the most recent interventions into the relationship between Muslims and the state, the community cohesion agenda may be the most short-lived but its impact has perhaps been the most profound. As a policy, the community cohesion agenda appears to have a limited life span. Many of the initiatives designed to facilitate community cohesion are still in place, especially in relation to schools, but funding associated with its presence in communities has been reduced or cut. Its impact lies not in any success it had in creating more cohesive societies nor in establishing strong relationships between Muslim and other groups but in the way the language and ideas associated with community cohesion quickly became the norm. Flint argues that as a policy it is insubstantial and short-lived but its legacy has been to consolidate and perpetuate the marginalisation of Islam in the UK (Flint and Robinson, 2008). In relation to the representation of Islam in education, community cohesion has consolidated a shift in the language and relationships associated with Islam through legitimising a raft of policies and initiatives from the Home Office that justified direct intervention into the teaching of issues to do with Islam. This first section of the chapter looks at how the community cohesion agenda presents Islam in the context of society and how the inclusion of schools as a significant factor in the strategy contributed to the processes described by Flint.

Many of the official documents and guidelines for community cohesion specifically identify Islam as a focus. For example *What Works in Community Cohesion*, the substantial research study produced by the Department for Communities and Local Government in 2007, mentions Muslims 33 times (Islam 6 times), Christians 6 times, Jews once and Hindus and Sikhs not at all. Community cohesion may have been commonly associated with Muslim communities but the official guidance for schools does not once mention Islam or Muslims. In 2006 the Education and Inspections Act inserted a new section into the 2002 Education Act, introducing a duty on the governing bodies of maintained schools to promote community cohesion. Guidance written by the DCSF notes that their proposals are rooted in existing legal duties for schools to eliminate unlawful racial discrimination, and to promote equality of opportunity and good relations between groups. The dominant theme in the guidance is the importance of a shared identity and a sense of belonging. It identifies the significant barriers to community cohesion as being the absence of a sense of belonging, the belief that other groups had priority, and community pride – but the nature of Muslim communities is never directly mentioned or referred to.

Identified as the main players in the project to create stronger communities, schools are requested to implement three key strategies. The first is for schools to build positive relationships between groups and pupils from different backgrounds, to reach out to parents, carers, families, school staff and community users of the school and its facilities and model the relationships you would expect to see in a strong community.

Secondly, schools can contribute to community cohesion through teaching. The guidance argues that in their curriculum schools should 'promote discussion of a common sense of identity' (DCSF, 2007). They should ensure that pupils are aware of human rights, that they develop the skills of participation and responsible action and that they can learn to value diversity. They cite examples of using assemblies, learning and teaching within Citizenship Education as well as whole school initiatives.

Thirdly, schools are required to establish links with the community beyond the school gates. They are encouraged to 'provide reasonable means for children, young people, their friends and families to interact with people from different backgrounds and to build positive relationships' (DCSF, 2007:7).

The guidance is detailed and comprehensive, yet Islam is wholly absent from the main body of the policy, its appendix and recommended resources and supplements. How is it that community cohesion is popularly associated with Islam and Muslim communities in some reports (Flint and Robinson, 2008) yet the guidance for schools does not mention them? The answer lies in the political context in which community cohesion became popularised and the ways in which communities and cohesion came to be understood in the language of policy and the language of schools and education.

Community cohesion – the background

At the heart of the relationship between community cohesion and UK Muslims is the assumption that Muslim communities have failed to integrate into British society. While other groups have adopted British values and customs, Muslims have apparently chosen to keep the traditions, values and customs of their families. A further assumption is that the failure of Muslims to integrate is problematic for the cohesiveness of modern British society. By not adopting British practices and beliefs, Muslims represent a weak link in the chain of communities that constitute a strong British society. The public nature of their rejection is often identified as one of the most problematic aspects of the failure to integrate (Robinson, 2008). While other communities may uphold the behaviour and values of their original cultures, they do it in private and confine it to realms that are usually considered peripheral to political life. Muslims by contrast are perceived to be consciously and publically rejecting British values through the way they dress, their sympathy for extremism, the status of women and the closed and geographically defined nature of the communities themselves (Ameli and Marandi, 2007).

The concept of integration is a key part of the cohesion agenda. *Our Shared Future* (Commission on Integration and Cohesion, 2007) refers to integration to improve relations between new migrants and the 'host society', and advocates 'cohesion' for closer relations between groups within society. However the two ideas are fused in the context of Islam in the UK and the political origins of that fusion lies in the disturbances of 2001.

During the summer of 2001 there were riots and civil disturbances in Bradford, Burnley, Oldham, Leeds and Stoke-on-Trent. They were immediately characterised as being due to the anger and frustration of Asian young men, even though white youth were also involved (Burnett, 2004). In Bradford the riots took place against a backdrop of a threatened National Front rally and tensions over the arrest of protesters.

Almost immediately the riots became the focus of a critique of race relations and, more specifically, of the segregation of Muslim communities as a result of the failure of previous strategies, notably multiculturalism. The Community Cohesion Team set up by the Labour government to investigate the underlying cause of the riots sent out task forces into the affected areas. The teams spoke to faith and community leaders and local residents and reviewed a variety of environments including schools, housing, recreation and places of worship.

The *Report of the Independent Review Team: Community Cohesion* identified cultural and social segregation as the main cause of the disturbances. In its list of key findings, the segregation of housing estates is placed first. The impact of segregation on the daily lives of communities in education, voluntary bodies, employment, worship and social and cultural events is emphasised. The Cantle Report, published in 2001, provided further exploration of the issues and identified the existence of segregated communities as a significant factor.

What is noticeable about the original report is that while it is this document that lays the basis for all further policy on community cohesion, Islam and Muslim communities are rarely mentioned. The executive summary opens with a quote from a Muslim of Pakistani origin who says 'When I leave this meeting with you I will go home and not see another white face until I come back here next week' (Home Office, 2001). There are numerous references to faith schools and one specific mention of Muslim schools. The most frequent allusion, however, is to a generic 'Asian' rather than a specific community.

The link between community cohesion and Islam in the UK is made not through the explicit referencing of Islam or events or examples that identify Muslims in the UK but by consistently referencing practices and situations that are already characterised as Islamic or associated with Muslims in some way. It is in this context that taking heed of the depth and range of associations made with Islam in public and popular discourses is essential to understanding how the representation of Islam is perpetuated. The process works through the constant allusion to debates and associations that are already established as referring to UK Muslims.

This is apparent in the way community cohesion is constructed and described in the Home Office report. In it, community cohesion is conceptualised as comprising several domains. All the domains: common values and civic culture; social order and social control; social solidarity and reductions in wealth disparities; social networks and social capital; place attachment and identity, could refer to any number of groups but most can be directly linked to the perceived nature of Muslim communities. The references to common values, tolerance, respect for difference, place attachments and identity are all themes that have been firmly established through the media and other discourses as characterising Islam or Muslim communities as political and social issues in the UK (Sheridan and Gillet, 2005). The report defines a problematic group as one that tends to live in a discrete geographical area, and visibly displays and publically articulates values and behaviour that are

70

not those of the majority in the UK, and are intolerant of others – in other words, a stereotypical portrayal of Muslim communities.

The area in which the invisible but obvious reference to Islam is most apparent in the discussion on education in relation to faith schools. The creation of Muslim schools has been a focus of tabloid and popular concern since the first one was planned. There are very few Muslim schools in the UK. In 2010, in a country with over 30,000 schools, there were about 100 independent and seven state schools which characterised themselves as Muslim. Their creation, their syllabus and ethos has generated a disproportionate amount of concern and attention, considering the number of pupils involved. A dominant theme in many of the discussions about Muslim schools is a fear that they encourage fundamentalism or a sense of separateness from the rest of UK society (Meer, 2007) and that, at worst, they act as a barrier to social cohesion (Tinker, 2009).

The belief that Muslim schools are possible sites of radicalism is implied in the Community Cohesion Report through association with previously established themes rather than explicit examples. The section on education begins by expressing concern that the quality of education is an issue in all the areas visited and the comment is made that it was often the case that 'faith based schools were favoured as much for their better than average results than for their faith based education' (Home Office, 2001:33), but the well published debates about Muslim schools are never explicitly mentioned. The report states that the creation of more faith schools would do nothing to break down the existing racial and ethnic segregation but would make the situation worse. It argues that schools should be doing more to challenge patterns of segregation rather than perpetuating them and that all schools, whether faith or non-faith, should seek to limit their intake from a single culture or ethnicity.

All these issues are associated with discussion about the legitimacy and desirability of increasing the number of Muslim schools. Ironically, the report mentions Christian schools more often than Muslim schools but comments about the dangers associated with monocultural schools are clearly a reference to the popular belief that Muslim schools encourage cultural segregation.

In terms of community cohesion, however a significant problem is posed by existing and future mono-cultural schools, which can add significantly to the separation of communities described above. The development of more faith based schools, may in some cases, lead to an increase in mono-cultural schools but this problem is not in any way confined to them. (Home Office, 2001:33)

The move towards community cohesion represents a significant shift in the way the state conceptualises race relations and therefore the way the state considers issues to do with equality and racial and ethnic discrimination (Tomlinson, 2008). The shift has been from an approach where differences between groups were accommodated in a multicultural framework to one where integration or assimilation into an agreed British framework of citizenship is now the only legitimate approach for groups and individuals wishing to be considered citizens (Worley, 2005) However, many of the ideas underpinning cohesion and integration had been gaining ground for some time. The ideas of the then Home Secretary, David Blunkett, on citizenship and identity were evident in the work of the team from the start. In *Politics and Progress* (2001), Blunkett drew on a popular American analysis of the relationship between social capital and social networks as the basis for strong links between groups. He argued that there was a link between the social activism of individuals, citizenship and the creation of common values that worked to underpin a shared nationhood.

The relationship between community cohesion and citizenship and the creation of common values is important in relation to UK Muslims because it serves to legitimise or criminalise certain types of communities. John Burnett argues that community as it is presented in the community cohesion agenda relies on a form of citizenship that focuses on obligations. The criterion for whether a community is legitimate or not is based on whether it carries out those obligations. Legitimate communities are those which carry out their obligations to the state and the wider society to which they belong. This idea of community means that good communities are those which have a positive relationship with initiatives and recommendations that demonstrate values shared with other groups. The implication, as Burnett argues, is that some communities refuse to follow a model of citizenship where civic pride and duty are key; these communities are viewed as a threat to the cohesiveness of society (Burnett, 2004). The idea is that some communities are deliberately segregating themselves from mainstream British society and this automatically means they are suspicious. Communities that deliberately position themselves outside the perimeters of the community cohesion agenda are legitimate targets for monitoring and surveillance.

The process by which ideas of community cohesion marginalise and criminalise UK Muslims is founded on particular ideas of belonging and the place of values in society. The emphasis on the importance of values is a key part of the way some communities are labelled as good and others are criminalised because they are perceived as rejecting liberal values. Values that are unacceptable, those thought of as undemocratic or anti-liberal, are identified as a salient factor in the creation of radicalised communities. At the same time, values that are pro-liberal, pro-democracy and British are considered an antidote to extremism and fundamentalism.

Community cohesion marginalises Muslim groups because it provides a narrative that identifies segregation or any meaningful difference in values and beliefs as anti-British (Flint and Robinson, 2008). The focus on values also serves to potentially criminalise all Muslims because Muslim beliefs which are considered to be 'distinctive' or 'fundamentalist' are conceived as expressions of values on a continuum of Islamic ideas with 'acceptable Muslim' ideas, at one end and their radical, extreme versions at the other.

As the next section shows, both the Labour and then the Coalition version of *Prevent* identify the lack of a national consensus or national value as a factor in creating an environment in which ideas of extremism flourish. In a speech at Cambridge University on 'Islam and Muslims in the world today', David Cameron argued that the London bombings were in part due to a 'sense of alienation' and a 'lack of belonging' particularly among British Muslims (Cameron, 2007). Chapter Five considers how the focus on values as both the cause of and the solution to extremism is a key part of the educational strategies for the teaching of issues relating to Islam.

RE and social cohesion

RE is the main curriculum area through which Islam is taught in schools and the way in which RE interprets the community cohesion agenda is key to understanding how Islam is represented in this context. Like all subjects, the factors that inform it are reflected in the debates that emanate from an academic community of specialists, and in the policies, publications and practices that relate to the professional and practical execution of the subject. In both areas, specialists involved in RE have been almost unanimous in their acceptance of community cohesion to the extent that is almost impossible to find any critique of it directed by RE specialists. The degree to which the RE community embrace it is indicated by the number of agreed syllabi that reference it, its recent inclusion in many RE textbooks and the dominance of materials promoting it on the Religious Education Council (REC) website.

In 2010, Michael Grimmitt published *Religious Education and Social and Community Cohesion*, an edited collection of essays written by leading scholars and specialists in the field of RE, Citizenship, faith schooling and political education. As a leading and influential writer in the field of RE for 30 years, and one who has been consistently critical of many aspects of RE, Grimmitt's book was expected to make a substantial contribution to the relationship between RE and community cohesion. Many of the chapters are critical but the common focus of their criticism is not the nature and assumptions underpinning community cohesion but the ability of RE to meet its demands.

The two final chapters written by Grimmitt himself illustrate this well. In the last chapter he examines 'some of the obstacles to RE fulfilling its requirement to contribute to social and community cohesion' (Grimmitt, 2010:260). He argues that in many respects RE is not able to contribute to this agenda. The legislation that underpins the teaching of RE undermines important educational principles because the RE curriculum must be 'disproportionately and discriminately weighted towards the study of Christianity for all pupils, irrespective of their family backgrounds' (p262). For Grimmitt, this one fact alone undermines the ability of RE to act as a vehicle for contributing to intercultural understanding and community cohesion. He goes on to argue that RE stands outside the 'equality agenda' of the last Labour government and that this is unlikely to change. His attack on the inability of RE to play a positive role in relation to the promotion of equality is unequivocal but nowhere does he challenge the social cohesion agenda. In fact he is clear that he supports it and that religious extremism is a significant issue that RE should address (p269).

Grimmitt's uncritical approach to community cohesion is mirrored in many of the other contributions to the collection. However, one of the most striking aspects is that, although this book represents RE's most systematic contribution to the discussion on community cohesion to date, a significant number of the writers make no mention of Islam. Some chapters focus on the nature of the agreed syllabi or the relationship between secularist and sacred interpretations of community but only a few discuss community cohesion in the context of debates around the nature of Islam, fundamentalism and religious extremism. As with many of the materials produced by REsilience, Islam is an invisible presence. In contrast, at the level of local guidance produced by the SACREs for the teaching of RE in schools, community cohesion is frequently and explicitly linked with Islam and extremism.

Like the chapters in Grimmitt's book, most agreed syllabi present the community cohesion agenda not just uncritically but enthusiastically. The Worcestershire agreed syllabus, for example, argues that RE has a key role to play in community cohesion because it can contribute positive messages about Islam that may work to challenge some of the stereotypes children encounter (Worcestershire Council, 2009). The agreed syllabus for the London Borough of Merton is even more explicit. In the opening letter, the Chair of the Council commends the syllabus to Merton schools 'with an expectation that it will cultivate a greater sense of community cohesion, through greater understanding and respect for the diversity of religions and cultures in the borough' (London Borough of Merton, 2008).

A curiosity of this debate is that there appears to be chasm of misunderstanding between those who believe that community cohesion has intensified and perpetuates discrimination against Muslims and those who believe that it represents an opportunity to facilitate equality and break down barriers between communities. It is important to recognise that neither proponents of community cohesion nor its critics constitute a coherent body of shared political interpretations.

The range of the critiques of community cohesion is equally far-reaching. Some commentators interpret the shift to community cohesion as a way of avoiding discussions about the poverty and discrimination faced by many Asian and Muslim groups (see eg. McGhee, 2003) while others argue that its assumptions about the nature of community essentialises Muslim groups and this perpetuates irreconcilable differences. Concepts of community that identify specific qualities and associate them with particular groups are rigid and monolithic and can be used to identify those communities which are legitimate and exclude others. The values associated with community as it is defined by the community cohesion agenda act as a benchmark by which Muslim communities can be evaluated and judged (Worley, 2005). What the critiques tend to share is a recognition that community cohesion disadvantages Muslim groups, that the agenda is informed by a desire to manage issues about race related issues rather than address the inequality experienced by Muslims in the UK (Khan, 2010).

The reason why specialists in RE have been reluctant to criticise community cohesion is unclear. One reading of the many agreed syllabi that support community cohesion principles is that they fully accept the premises of the community cohesion agenda. Most interpretations and models of community cohesion that appear in the agreed syllabi could have been taken directly from the Denham report, the substantial government report into the riots of 2001. Most agreed syllabi imply that radical extremism is a significant issue, that an absence of shared values is problematic, that there really are segregated communities which need persuading to relate to wider British society and that creating greater contact between these communities is a positive move.

Another possible reason is that even though individuals may be aware of the contested nature of community cohesion, they believe that it is more productive to work within the structure and guidelines of community cohesion than to stand aloof from the process. There is a long tradition in RE of positioning its resources and the aims of its teaching as part of a wider educational approach to the promotion of equality, the celebration of diversity and the cultivation of tolerance between different cultures and groups (Arthur, Gearon and Sears, 2010). It may be that many specialists in RE believe that although the community cohesion agenda is flawed RE still has a great deal to offer in the way it represents Islam through education. It is more productive to engage with the agenda than to reject it completely.

We can see this process at work in the guidelines produced by the RE Council of Great Britain about RE and Community Cohesion. Although the report reminds readers that community cohesion is only one of the many aims of RE, the opening sentence states that the REC is committed to supporting schools and educational institutions in promoting it. The report takes great care not to focus on Islam or Muslim communities, stating that the requirements apply to *all* communities. Pre-empting many of the criticisms of community cohesion, it stresses the fluid, dynamic and diverse nature of communities and states that this is an opportunity for RE to engage pupils in the notion of shared values and the recognition of their existence as part of a global community (REC, 2010:9).

Yet this process has sometimes been problematic. RE frequently competes with Citizenship Education where it seeks to engage pupils in more critical reflections on the role and impact of religion in people's lives (Grimmitt, 2010). To locate its place in the curriculum, RE possibly seeks to reaffirm its role as a subject area that can provide pupils with the skills they need in modern society. However the absence in RE of any recognition of the debates that accuse community cohesion of actively discriminating against Muslims raises concerns about the independent nature of RE. If one of the aims of RE is truly to help pupils develop the skills they need to combat prejudice and stereotyping then it is surprising that it should have wholeheartedly embraced a strategy that has been so controversial.

Not surprisingly, the chapters in Grimmitt's book that criticise the community cohesion agenda do so from the perspective of citizenship education (Osler, 2010), political/philosophy education (Gearon, 2010), an Islamic educational perspective (Sahin, 2010) or faith (Thompson, 2010). Although these chapters are very different, they all question the meaning and significance of community cohesion.

It is likely that RE specialists would rather their subject be a part of a community cohesion agenda than have no role. However, this raises questions about the way RE presents Islam and Muslim communities through the curriculum and about the way RE defines itself as a curriculum subject. The examination below of the relationship between RE and the *Prevent* strategy reveals that RE has become integrated into a wider counter-terrorism strategy that makes questionable assumptions about the nature and significance of Islam as a religion and as a focus for extremism.

Contest and *Prevent*

Islam is no longer just a curriculum subject taught and learned about by pupils in the context of a syllabus or curriculum guidelines – it is now a political issue. The associations between Islam and radicalisation, social disintegration, extremism and national security as well as between Islam and cultural and community practices are interpreted in popular discourse as an affront to Britishness. Islam has assumed significance in education that goes beyond traditionally taught RE lessons and the representation of Islam in schools should take account of these wider debates. Recent policies have created an ideological and policy framework within education which shapes and distorts any discussion of Islam.

The 9/11 and 7/7 bombings provoked anger in the British government. Its responses appeared based on the assumption that Muslims were a threat and were unwilling to embrace British norms. Liz Fekete likens the political climate to a 'new McCarthyism'; it generates fear and suspicion of Islam and Muslims. It sees them as a threat to national security, while at the same time it legitimises the monitoring and regulation of Muslims and Muslim communities (Fekete, 2009).

The new McCarthyism is evident in the Home Office response to the 7/7 bombings. First came the increased willingness of politicians and public figures to challenge multiculturalism. Then came increased hostility to refugees and asylum seekers.

Home Secretary David Blunkett argued that people who came to settle in the UK needed to do more to 'foster a sense of belonging', insinuating that Muslim communities deliberately pursued a strategy of non-integration. He introduced a policy of 'Integration with Diversity' that included proposals to speed up deportation and tests for the language skills of new immigrants. David Gillborn (2008) described the policy as characterised by a return to an assimilationist/integrationalist position that makes a causal link between communities that have failed to integrate and radicalisation.

These assumptions were made explicit in the discussions facilitated by the media and public opinion. The constant negative media coverage depicting Muslims as intolerant and anti-British, and Islam as a religion prone to extremism, violence and inequality generated suspicion of Muslims and violence against them (Abbas, 2011). It was in this climate that the Labour Government initiated a strategy to establish a process of monitoring, while regulating attitudes towards Islam and Muslims through a network of relationships between schools, faith groups, the voluntary sector and the criminal justice system. The government called its counter terrorism strategy *Contest* and the strategy set up to provide and maintain this network for halting the spread and rise of extremism was called *Prevent.*

I argue that that there is a relationship between the representation of Islam in education and the way Islam is conceived in official policy and public debates. The way in which Islam is located as a threat to national security powerfully affects how it is represented in other arenas, including education.

At the time of writing, the Home Office estimates that the threat level in the UK from international terrorism is severe – that is, a terrorist attack is 'highly likely' (Home Office, 2011:5). It organises counter-terrorism around four distinct workstreams, each with its own objectives:

- Pursue: to stop terrorists attacks
- Prevent: to stop people becoming terrorists or supporting terrorism
- Protect: to strengthen our protection against a terrorist attack; and
- Prepare: to mitigate the impact of a terrorist attack

Contest was first developed by the Government in 2003 and again in 2008 when these four strands were introduced. *Prevent* is intended to organise communities so they can better oppose or resist ideologies of violent extremism and it has drawn criticism mainly because of the way it has targeted Muslims. Consequently, the new version of *Prevent* had a widened remit for communities to be supported in their development and promotion of shared values.

In 2010, Liberty, the UK's foremost civil liberties and human rights organisation, published its criticism of *Prevent*. Liberty pointed out that it simultaneously stigmatises the Muslim community as a whole while failing to address the threat of violence created by forms of extremism with no link to Islam. It demanded that the government stop using Islamic theology as a marker to determine whether Muslim communities were extremist or not. Liberty argued that *Prevent* initiatives had in some cases not only discriminated against Muslims but had used strategies that resulted in the alienation of entire communities and which could be considered 'as likely to fall foul of both equality and human rights law' (Liberty, 2010:7).

Arun Kundnani, editor of the journal *Race and Class*, published a report funded by the Joseph Rowntree Charitable Trust: *Prevent: Spooked! How not to prevent violent extremism*. Like the Liberty report, *Spooked* criticised the government for using theology as a criterion for sponsorship and for alienating communities where good work was already in progress. And, like the Liberty report, it focuses on the way the entire Muslim population is constructed through *Prevent* as a 'suspect community'. Kundnani describes *Prevent* not a community-driven project where groups determine their own priorities but a process where local authorities have been pressurised to accept *Prevent* funding in direct proportion to the number of Muslims in their area to ensure that all Muslims fall within the scope of *Prevent* monitoring and regulation (Kundnani, 2009:6).

Other commentators assert that *Prevent* is counter-productive because it creates suspicion and hostility between groups. In *The Prevent Strategy and Controversies* (2010), Heather Marshall criticises *Prevent* for dismantling existing good relations between communities and government authorities, rather than creating resilience in communities against radicalism.

Many Muslims have attacked the *Prevent* strategy. The An-Nisa Society argues in *Preventing Violent Extremism* (PVE) and *Prevent – A Response from the Muslim Community* that the entire strategy is flawed (Khan, 2009:3). It asserts that *Prevent* has led to a disproportionate criminalisation of Muslims through its assumption that all 'Muslims are vulnerable by virtue of the fact that they are members of a Muslim community'. It objects to *Prevent*'s language: the term 'violent extremism' is used as effectively synonymous with Muslim groups. This, they say, criminalises all Muslims and, moreover, ignores the fact of security threats from groups such as the far right.

The first *Prevent* programme, established in 2008, was conceived as the part of *Contest* which would actively seek to establish relationships with community partners as a way of 'stopping people becoming or supporting terrorists and violent extremism' (Home Office, 2008). This original strategy included five themes and key objectives that were designed to help communities combat the threat of terrorism. The underlying principle of all the themes is that individuals become terrorists through a combination of social and religious isolation that makes them vulnerable to ideologies that can lead to supporting or being involved in terrorism. The five themes are:

- Challenging violent extremism
- Disrupting the promotion of violent extremism
- Supporting susceptible and vulnerable individuals who are thought to be likely targets of radicalisation
- Increasing the capacity of communities to resist ideologies that promote violent extremism
- Addressing the grievances which ideologues are exploiting

The rewritten *Prevent* of 2011 styled itself as more direct and focused in its monitoring of the factors leading to extremism. The Foreword stated that the original version had failed to confront extremist ideology and had confused government policy to promote integration with government policy to prevent terrorism. It said that it had been neither rigorous nor effective enough in its strategies to prevent the growth of extremism. This updated strategy promised to be more 'robust' in its monitoring and 'to do more than any other government before us to promote integration'. It declared that 'governance will be strengthened at every level' (Home Office, 2011).

The twin aims of promoting integration and preventing terrorism are even more closely linked. The authors believe that extremist ideas are the foundation of terrorism. They assert that these ideas are more likely to thrive where there is a 'rejection of a cohesive, integrated, multi-faith society and of parliamentary democracy' (Home Office, 2011:5). Rejection of common values or the desirability of a cohesive society, they claim, creates the possibility for the growth of extremism. Extremist ideas, which they define as those which reject a cohesive society, will be less likely to thrive where a strong sense exists of belonging to 'this country' and having 'support for our core values'. The implication is clear. Groups and communities that do not demonstrate support for core values or exhibit a sense of belonging are vulnerable to extremist ideologies. According to the criteria laid out in *Prevent*, these communities, organisations or groups are therefore acceptable targets for monitoring, regulation and intervention (Home Office, 2011).

The monitoring and regulation of Muslim communities is legitimised through the potential threat they pose by their very difference. *Prevent* is careful to differentiate between what it refers to as 'legitimate religious belief' and extremist ideas, but the report is explicit that it considers any ideas which do not support core values or community cohesion as potentially extremist. Whether or not a religious belief (or any belief) is legitimate is not, for *Prevent,* a theological or philosophical question. What matters is whether it articulates a sense of belonging to the UK or can be included in the core values identified by the Home Office.

The *Prevent* strategies identify education as a site of vulnerability and of resistance to extremism, although teachers may be surprised to learn that they are placed at the forefront of a government campaign to prevent terrorism. The *Prevent* strategy targets education as a key area of concern and as a significant contributor in its plans to stop the growth of radicalisation. *Prevent* acknowledges that there has been 'no systematic attempt to recruit or radicalise people in full time education' but points to cases where individuals who support terrorist groups or ideologies have been employed in schools. *Prevent* is also interested that schools and lessons provide an environment where the ideas underpinning terrorism can be addressed directly with pupils and countered. The Strategy describes a scenario where school engagement with *Prevent* is already substantial; it lists eleven initiatives that it has funded and promoted, including:

- A DfE authored toolkit designed to help schools fight violent extremism, with guidelines for schools on how best to develop an ethos that champions democratic values and human rights
- A DfE workbook that links *Prevent* to other school safety and improvement policies – accompanied by grants of over £5.6 million to embed the approaches
- The publication in 2009 by the Association of Chief Police Officers (ACPO) of guidance entitled 'Prevent, Police and Schools' to enable police officers to work more effectively with schools and teachers
- The production of a DVD box set called 'Watch Over Me' funded by the ACPO, DfE and the Office for Security and Counter Terrorism. This has been sent out to every secondary school in England and has been accompanied by training events organised for teachers, police officers and community workers
- The funding of the Religious Education Council of England and Wales by the DfE, DfESF and the Department for Communities and Local Government to deliver the *RE*silience project to help teachers of RE discuss contentious issues including extremism

The scope and range of government intervention in education in relation to extremism and its links with Islam constitutes a coherent and systematic framework that effectively criminalises aspects of theology, education, cultural practices and community that are associated with Islam. Within the *Prevent* document every area of British Muslim life, the Madrash, Muslim neighbourhoods, the Mosque and after-school clubs attended by Muslim children are all mentioned as potential sites of risk from radicalisation.

Furthermore, *Prevent* criminalises British Islam by citing many of the aspects of behaviour and beliefs associated with Islam as descriptors for vulnerability to radicalisation. The qualities of belonging, participation, community and identification with UK civic society are repeatedly cited as major bulwarks against radicalisation. Therefore it must be the case, it maintains, that individuals, families or groups who do not identify with UK civic society or choose not to participate or demonstrate their belonging to UK society are vulnerable to radicalisation.

This logic informs the *Learning together to be safe* toolkit published by the DCSF as part of *Prevent* in 2008. The toolkit focuses on the ways schools can work with pupils to prevent violent extremism. It shows teachers how they can develop curricula that challenge extremism and use strategies that encourage honest and frank debate about even the most sensitive issues. A debate held in two Burnley schools in Lancashire around the statement 'One man's freedom fighter is another man's terrorist' is given as an example of pupil engagement in controversial but relevant discussions. The debates were the culmination of a six week programme of research and discussion on figures such as Osama Bin Laden, Martin McGuiness, Martin Luther King and Nelson Mandela and culminated in a formal debate where 'Muslim and Christian students really enjoyed sharing views and beliefs in a safe and respectful environment' (DCSF, 2008:30).

Such activities can undoubtedly be enormously valuable for pupils. It is not these lessons or activities that I challenge, but the context and issues identified by the toolkit. The introduction notes that while terrorism has often been a feature of British life, its form has changed – that twenty years ago it would have been 'Irish terrorism' but today it is mostly 'violent extremism influenced by Al Qaida'. Pupils and teachers are left in no doubt that every issue they discuss in these programmes concerning threats to security is in the context of Islam.

The toolkit uses the phrase 'extremist narratives', thus implying a world that is violent, threatening and aggressive, yet the factors that are seen to constitute an extremist narrative are surprisingly general. It suggests that teachers and pupils should be able to recognise the narratives used by extremists or those likely to be vulnerable to extremism to describe their lives and identifies a range of narratives individuals might use to explain their lives that, it believes, could indicate their vulnerability to extremism. The examples it offers of narratives that are features of extremism or which may lead to extremism are those which set out:

■ To explain why I/my family/my community am/are experiencing disadvantage/suffering/lack of respect eg perceived persecution, inequality, oppression by a governing class, national or international politics

- To explain why the conventional family/school/community solutions do not provide answers to the core grievances eg 'the law does not protect us, my family is isolated from 'real life' and does not know what it is like for young people'

- And then go on to justify violent or criminal remedies – either in local, or national settings e g 'we need to force a change of views, the only way to achieve change is through action' or 'we need to avenge the wrong we have suffered'

- In some cases the cause is part of a wider global movement which may claim a political, ideological or theological basis, however distorted (DCSF, 2008:16)

Significantly these narratives, especially the first two, could apply to thousands of families and individuals who have experienced discrimination, disadvantage or inequality and have attributed the cause of that discrimination to the way society works. In effect, *Prevent* suggests that anyone who believes that the inequality that exists in society should be vigorously challenged and that legal and social justice have failed them is vulnerable to radicalisation. By this definition all Muslims in the UK who have ever experienced racism or discrimination or have been disappointed by the behaviour towards them of the local police, school or council are potential purveyors or victims of 'extremist narratives'.

The toolkit lists other still more general characteristics that might render individuals vulnerable to exploitation by violent extremists, such as

- identity crisis
- personal crisis
- personal circumstances
- unemployment or underemployment
- criminality

Again, the salient feature of these categories is their breadth. They are so general that, taken out of the context of a document dedicated to teaching about Islamic radicalisation and extremism, they could be descriptors for adolescents everywhere. In the context of *Prevent*'s stated focus, all these characteristics could be taken as describing young Muslims' possible lives. The paragraph attached to the second point is especially telling, stating that:

The experiences of migration, local tensions or events affecting families in countries of origin may contribute to alienation from UK values and a decision to cause harm to symbols of the community or state. (DCSF, 2008:18)

It is also revealing that the only language other than English in which the report is available on the Home Office website is Arabic and that it is only Islam that is repeatedly named and used as an example throughout the document.

There is no way of knowing how thoroughly *Prevent* is now embedded in schools. The Home Office believes that schools are all aware of the Strategy and that local authorities are increasingly recognising *Prevent* as an important tool for protecting young people from radicalisation. A survey conducted by Ipsos MORI in 2011 indicated that a majority of schools (84%) recognise that they have a role in preventing terrorism and most (75%) regard this role as important. A significant minority (20%) disagreed and 70 per cent of schools felt they needed more training to build resilience to radicalisation (Phillips, Tse and Johnson, 2010). It may be that many schools do not regard challenging extremism a priority, but knowing that the government acts on the belief that there is a relationship between extremism, Islam and values in education has implications for Islam in the curriculum. It is this knowledge that compromises the last initiative I analyse, *RE*silience, and its chances of success in furthering understanding of Muslims.

*RE*silience

Of the many initiatives promoted by the Home Office in relation to Islam, *RE*silience has been the least challenged. *Contest, Prevent* and the community cohesion agenda have all been criticised for the way they can work to criminalise Muslims (Bartlett and Birdwell, 2010) or for being founded on political and philosophical assumptions that Islam is associated with extremism and the failure of Muslim communities to integrate. *RE*silience, though, conceived as an integral part of *Contest* and *Prevent,* has so far escaped such criticism. Instead, it has successfully presented itself as promoting equality and diversity through education about tolerance and engagement with contentious issues.

Yet many of the criticisms levelled against *Prevent* and *Contest* remain valid for *RE*silience, even though the educationalists who developed

*RE*silience or who use it in schools may be striving to represent Islam fairly. The lens through which *RE*silience filters all knowledge about Islam and radicalism is irredeemably coloured by what Kincheloe calls 'dominant epistemological perspectives', perspectives which ignore 'the impact of Western colonialism/neo-colonialism on the relationship between the Islamic world and the West' (Kincheloe, 2010:95). Gateway materials introduce teachers to some areas that are considered critically but the fact that every aspect of the West's relationship with the Muslim world is premised on inequality and domination is never taken into account.

The location of *RE*silience within a pedagogical framework based on practices common in RE allows the approaches and ideas in the Gateways to be used positively by teachers as stand-alone lessons or activities. The Gateways provide substantial blocs of knowledge that could be invaluable to all teachers. However, as part of a strategy to build resilience against radicalism and extremism *RE*silience is founded on the same assumptions as *Prevent* and *Contest* – assumptions we have seen to be informed by Islamophobia.

The main objectives of *RE*silience are those also of *Prevent*. They are presented as part of the wider Home Office strategy to work with key organisations which could intervene in the protection of those who are vulnerable to extremist ideologies. *Prevent* argues that because the young are particularly vulnerable to exploitation and because educational sites offer teachers opportunities to address key issues of terrorism, civic responsibility and citizenship directly, education is a key part of this strategy. A number of organisations bid for the tender to develop materials and resources and the RE Council won the contract. But they did not start with a clean sheet. Many of the political assumptions underpinning *Contest* and *Prevent*, and some of the assumptions about the nature of Islam and Muslims promoted by the Home Office, became part of the work developed by the RE Council.

The RE Council is essentially the public face of the RE community in the UK. It works with teachers, faith groups, university lecturers and specialised campaigns and projects in developing and promoting RE. The organisation acts as a voice for Religious Education in the media and in meetings with government bodies. *RE*silience was the latest in a raft of measures introduced by the Labour Government in response to developments which involved Islam. The attacks on the Twin Towers, the bombings in London by British-born Muslims and the riots and disturbances in northern towns in 2001 all served to reinforce the government's idea that Muslim communities in the UK were vulnerable to exploitation and the attractions of a radicalised, fundamentalist, anti-Western Islam. The winning of a contract funded by the Department for Children, Schools and Families (DCSF) was a significant coup for RE – it confirmed that RE had a positive role to play in combating extremism and, as Islam became increasingly politicised, that RE had a significant role too in challenging the way ethnic minority and religious communities were stereotyped in popular discourse.

REsilience was designed to support teachers who engage with contentious and controversial issues. The resources offer advice, subject knowledge, and individualised support for teachers wishing to develop a practical action plan in their school. The extensive materials were commissioned to provide in-depth information, lists of relevant publications and resources and key questions for debate and reflection, in a series of 'Gateways' to particular issues.

Although REsilience is part of the *Contest* stable of initiatives, it differs from them in important ways. The attitudes it promotes are in line with those of RE more generally and its engagement with the issues is justified in educational terms. The materials are informed by underlying philosophical and educational assumptions and a pedagogy that would be familiar to any specialist in RE. Each Gateway approaches a specific issue from the standpoint of all or some of the recognised attitudes in Religious Education, as outlined in the *Non-Statutory Framework for Religious Education* (QCA, 2004:13). Thus there is consistent emphasis on enabling teachers to create a classroom environment where all views are listened to and a safe space is afforded pupils in which to discuss their opinions. The importance of allowing students to develop their own opinions and responses is emphasised throughout the Gateway materials. They give teachers the opportunity to explore debates that may challenge assumptions about Islam and radicalisation embedded in other *Contest* and *Prevent* resources. Suggestions to help teachers encourage pupils to respect all cultures and religious practices, as well as guidance on how teachers can adopt a neutral stance in their teaching, appear in Gateway 2.1 and Gateway 2.4: *Demonstrating respect for cultures and religions – Adopting an impartial stance while teaching*. The established tradition in RE of teacher neutrality and objectivity in relation to all religions and religious practices and beliefs is echoed and reinforced in the Gateway documents. Teachers are advised that:

> even when views are discussed or voiced that are against the law or in breach of the school's code of conduct this should not preclude serious discussion about whether certain laws or aspects of a code of conduct are unjust or inappropriate and in need of reform. (Gateway, 2.1 and 2.4:2)

*RE*silience affirms the central role of teachers as to cultivate the skills pupils need to negotiate views and values different from their own rather than to impose different values on others. Teachers may on occasion play devil's advocate but it is not their job to regulate or change pupils' opinions because those views oppose the law or criticise the legal system. Teachers are reminded that the values of pupils are especially important in the secondary phase precisely because this is the time when they are developing world views that might inform the rest of their lives and when they 'need to feel that their opinion is as worthy of being heard as that of the teacher' (Gateway, 2.1 and 2.4:2). Unlike other documents produced under the *Contest* remit, there is rarely a suggestion that teachers should be steering pupils or young people towards an official or legitimate view of Islam, Muslims or even of radicalisation. The Gateways remind teachers that the 'ethos of RE embodies respect for all members of the student community' and that the space for open debate provided in the RE classroom should 'be available when work involves issues like those included in *RE*silience' (Gateway, 2.2:1). Gateway 2.2: *Displaying sensitivity to the home backgrounds and the beliefs of pupils* argues that prior knowledge of the students' religious background is important when teaching *RE*silience issues, citing as examples that teachers should be aware that some Muslim or Jewish students may be particularly sensitive when the topic under discussion is the Israel/Palestine conflict, and that Hindu and Muslim students may be similarly sensitive about discussions of the continuing dispute over the sovereignty of Kashmir.

Secondly, the use in *RE*silience of words and phrases which signify Islam or Muslims is far less evident than in the materials produced by

Contest or *Prevent*. Even when addressing issues that are commonly associated with Islam in the public imagination, Islam is rarely used as an exemplar. In Gateway Document 4.9: *Violence towards women, especially when given a religious justification,* there is no mention of Islam apart from a brief sentence in the section on forced marriage and in the final lists of books and websites for further reading. References are made to families in the Middle East, North Africa or Asia and to practices carried out in North East Africa but mention of Islam or Muslims is largely avoided.

This Gateway document specifically looks at 'honour crimes', female genital mutilation and forced marriage and it acknowledges that these practices are frequently justified on religious grounds. Where Islam is mentioned, the document stresses that 'it is important to emphasise that forced marriage is not a teaching of any religion' and quotes a statement by the Muslim Parliament of Great Britain that under Islamic and UK law, mutual consent is always a prerequisite to marriage.

Neither is reference made to Islam in discussions about the handling of issues where sensitivity is required. In *Displaying sensitivity to the home backgrounds and the beliefs of pupils,* Gateway 2.2 identifies challenges that might arise in the classroom as a result of inflamed tensions, such as when students and their parents who hold extreme views object to the neutral stance of the RE teacher, or when terrorists attacks are reported in the local and national press that might inflame relations between students. Again, there is no mention of Islam nor a suggestion that any of the listed challenges to teachers are prompted by events that involve Muslims. Teachers are advised to make sure they are alert to world and national affairs and that they are always open about the content of the RE syllabus, but it is never suggested that knowledge about the geopolitical significance of Islam or the domestic politics involving Muslim communities might be particularly useful for teachers.

Thirdly, *RE*silience's publications are as a rule more detailed and thorough than those produced by *Contest* and *Prevent*. Moreover, the material is organised so as to provide teachers with substantial theological or historical background material for many of the topics. Each Gateway starts with a section explaining how each issue is relevant to Resilience, then lists and discusses key questions that will support pupil engagement with the main points while also helping teachers to maintain the focus of their teaching. The Gateway explains why the issues featured are contentious and outlines the challenges likely to occur in a RE classroom.

All Gateways have signposts for further reading, resources and action and most have appendices that constitute substantial chunks of background knowledge. Gateway Document 4.3c, *Religion and Conflict: Partition and its aftermath*, is a good example of the depth in which some of the documents discuss the issues. It provides teachers with ten pages of analysis, historical context and links to how issues arising from the partition of India might relate to the identity of pupils of Indian, Pakistani or Bangladeshi heritage. In the appendix, the roots of partition in British colonialism and the pre-colonial relationship between Islam and the Indian subcontinent are described in some detail. It offers not only differing political and partisan viewpoints but also consideration of the historical and contemporary consequences of partition for Muslims, Sikhs and Hindus.

Fourthly, the materials produced by *RE*silience differ from the two earlier initiatives in the care they take not to generalise about Muslim traditions or religious beliefs. Certain ideas and practices are linked, where appropriate, to specific Muslim denominations or national and cultural customs. When a contentious or controversial issue is raised and examples are given, Islam is rarely the only context for the example. So Gateway 4.4 on *Hatred based on religion, ethnicity or 'race' especially when given religious justification* begins its analysis by problematising the concepts of race and ethnicity and then analysing the roots of the discussion in the European mid 19th Century discourses on racial types and discourses on, for instance, the existence of the caste system in India. Where race hatred based on religion is addressed, it touches on that shown by Al Qaida, but only as part of a wider discussion on extremism that includes the activities of the English Defence League.

Fifthly, and uniquely amongst all *Contest* related materials, only *RE*silience considers the impact of discrimination and hatred against Muslims as part of the remit of contentious or controversial issues. In Gateway 4.4, teachers are reminded that any form of stereotyping is harmful, including stereotyping Muslims or regarding the community of Islam as one homogenous entity:

Teachers of RE can help students to become more aware that most Muslims are not terrorists or supporters of terrorist activity and that stereotyping of particular ethnic, cultural and religious groups is unjust and damaging to all concerned. For most Muslims, the sense of being a member of the ummah, or worldwide community of Muslims, is an important part of their identity, for some it may be the most important part, but this is a situation mirrored in other religions and loyalty to a transnational religious grouping is in no way incompatible with loyalty to a nation state. (Gateway 4.4:3)

It is this willingness to consider the possibility that Muslims in the UK have experienced discrimination and prejudice because of a climate of accusation and hostility towards them that sets *REsilience* apart from other *Contest* documents and is its foremost strength. Its weakness, however, stems from approaching Islam in the same way as the RE textbooks do: through the world religions prism (see Chapter Three). There is the same implicit insistence that Islam is just another religion and that the experience of Muslims and Muslim pupils is no different from that of pupils from other ethnic minority groups or other faiths.

Thus the neutral and objective stance recommended by the Gateways in line with a standard RE ethos reinforces an approach that in effect de-radicalises Islam and presents it as one religion among many. An approach that effectively relativises the representation of Islam restricts opportunities for teachers and pupils to engage with sufficient of the narratives that situate Islam as a source of terror and extremism.

*RE*silience and the invisible Islam

The assumptions that the sacred core of world religions enriches human existence and that the daily practice of religious beliefs and rituals is a positive aspect of human culture and community is reflected in the way *RE*silience documents stress the need for teachers to cultivate respect for religions and religious beliefs. Targeting Islam as a particular source of contentious issues or directly associating Muslim communities with radicalisation or extremism would sit uncomfortably with the main-stream RE ethos of neutrality and objectivity and the assumption that world religions should be treated equally.

Because the *Contest* initiatives were developed and written some years earlier, the RE Council and the authors of the Gateways would have known about the criticism levelled at the *Contest* and *Prevent* strategies and community cohesion agenda before they bid for the contract, and certainly before they started developing the materials. They cannot fail to have been aware that many Muslim groups in Universities and colleges, local community groups and national Muslim organisations had objected that some of the *Contest* initiatives were intrusive and Islamophobic and had expressed their suspicions about both the motivation for and the potential impact of *Prevent* and Community Cohesion.

To some extent the Gateway resources set *RE*silience apart from the others in the government programme because they are rooted in an RE context. But this context does not ensure that *RE*silience is distanced from the assumptions about Islam embedded in *Contest*; it often reinforces and perpetuates them. I try to analyse why an initiative designed to be positive in its representation of Islam and to be sympathetic and neutral in its discussion of contentious issues that relate to *Prevent* should end up consolidating some of the familiar pejorative assumptions.

Omission and context

A recent debate in RE has focused on the way RE as a curriculum subject represents religions as lived social and cultural entities. Specialists in the representation of religion in RE have questioned the tendency to present a preferred model of religion through a selective choice of facts, images and beliefs (Barnes, 2007; Wright; 2004; Panjwani, 2005). The last chapter showed how religion tends to be misrepresented because of a desire to promote a model that reinforces a particular outlook and not because of any wish to demonise it. But whatever the motives for misrepresentation of a religion, some of the tactics are the same – and first among them is omission.

Mirroring an approach embedded in the ideas and pedagogies that underpin RE causes the assumptions behind the teaching of Islam in RE to be reproduced. This perpetuates two distinct but related approaches. The first ignores the disengagement with certain social and political contexts; the second ignores narratives or issues which challenge the liberal interpretation of religion.

93

Although omission can be understood as a passive tool in the way religions are portrayed, the effect is troubling, especially when the omissions relate to widely held public discourse. This is certainly the case with Islam and many of the Gateway documents. Any teacher turning to *RE*silience for resources and information about *Prevent* related issues would expect them to focus on Islam but they seldom do. Omitting Islam from many of the examples given in the Gateways could be due to the desire to redress the vilification of Islam in so much popular discourse or even in other *Contest* related documents. But all it does is highlight the discrepancy between what is written in the Gateways and what is already presumed and dominates as public knowledge.

The omission of Islam distorts discussions and creates a disconcerting vacuum. For example, Gateway 2.2, *Displaying sensitivity to the home backgrounds and the beliefs of pupils* addresses the challenges teachers may face when they teach about issues that relate to the community or family history of certain children. It lists these challenges, among them that:

- students and their parents who hold extreme views might object to the positive and respectful stance taken towards all religions and to non-religious world views
- reports in the local and national press – of terrorist attacks, for instance – might inflame relations between groups of students
- students from specific religions might feel uncomfortable or under threat when an issue raised concerns a controversial aspect of their faith

The document addresses most of these challenges by providing strategies and ideas that can be introduced as part of classroom practice. Gateway 2.2 recommends that teachers be open with parents and families about their approach and the character and content of the RE curriculum, and suggests that parents who have relevant specialised knowledge could be invited to share their expertise with the rest of the class or school. When relations between pupils have been inflamed because of a terrorist attack teachers should decide whether events have local resonance and then possibly suspend planned lessons and 'invite discussion of the event in the informed and well managed surroundings of the classroom' (Gateway, 2.2). A teacher turning to *RE*silience for support could reasonably expect that material designed to address strategies for dealing with tensions caused by a terrorist attack to mention Islam as at least one of the examples, yet there is no mention whatever of Islam in this section. The Gateway authors probably wanted to avoid reinforcing the stereotypical association between Islam and terrorism.

However, the method the authors chose for challenging this stereotype appears to be to disengage with the issue rather than looking at the assumptions and ideology behind it. Opting for omission leaves existing prejudices intact and fails to provide alternative facts, arguments and worldviews that could challenge Islamophobia and stop pupils from inevitably making connections of their own between Muslims and terrorism. The important topic of Gateway 2.2 argues that teachers should seek to invite discussion that is well informed – but it does not give teachers the arguments or the materials to do this.

Consequently Islam is represented in the Gateways not by association with radicalisation or extremism as it is in *Contest* and *Prevent*, but through conspicuous absence, a negative space. These spaces may escape reiterating prejudices against Islam but they do nothing to challenge the associations that already exist in the minds of pupils and teachers. While the emphasis is on encouraging honest and well-informed discussions in which pupils will feel safe enough to articulate their beliefs, pre-existing ideas or associations between Islam, Muslims and radicalisation are not consistently addressed.

The opening quote of this chapter refers to the place of RE as an integral part of the *Prevent* agenda. The agenda has, however, alienated many Muslims, criminalised Islam, legitimised government regulation of Muslim theology and in some cases destroyed existing community relationships. The fact that this agenda is reformulated for the classroom through *RE*silience or reinterpreted by RE teachers may mean that Islam as presented in schools through *Prevent* is given a different spin that can appear positive. Gateway materials provide guidance that supports teachers in developing lessons that encourage pupils to consider different perspectives. *RE*silience presents many contentious issues from a variety of angles and often in significant depth.

But however carefully and fully *RE*silience encourages pupils to think about issues, this does not mean that the representations of Islam perpetuated by the Home Office or the media are openly challenged or that the most salient issues and factors that shape the lives of contemporary Muslims are addressed. This is not because teachers are consciously following the dictates of the Home Office or because all teachers agree with *Prevent* (although some do) but because many of the assumptions underpinning *Contest* about values and radicalisation are also ingrained in education. The educational and social context in which *RE*silience is used is bound to fill the gaps which exist in its materials and consequently to compromise their effect.

5

Tolerance and Representation

To meet the standards that define their professional conduct, teachers will be required from September 2012 not 'to undermine fundamental British values'. Teachers will be expected to promote 'British values' throughout their careers.

Islam is represented in education in ways that are sometimes subtle and invisible but in the case of the new standards for teachers the representation is direct. The Department for Education states that the definition of fundamental British values is taken from the 'definition articulated in the new *Prevent* strategy', and that this includes democracy, the rule of law, individual respect and tolerance of different faiths and beliefs (DfE, 2011:4). Thus the standards that articulate the behaviour and attitudes of teachers incorporate a model of national identity in which Muslim values and communities have been identified as problematic. That the Department of Education should couch their requirement in the language of tolerance and respect is indicative of the complex ways in which Islam is represented.

This closing chapter argues that the call for educators, pupils and students to cultivate tolerance towards Islam may appear progressive but that it could be seen, rather, as a recent form of Orientalism. A call for tolerance marks new boundaries between 'them' and 'us', defined by a specific relation to toleration, and it assumes a fundamental difference between 'us' and 'Islam'. Educationalists who aim to engage with Islam in the classroom in ways that are not Islamophobic may find my criticism of current practice frustrating, but when government is increasingly insistent that communities assimilate and integrate, when 'fundamental British values' are part of compulsory schooling and when Muslims are continually vilified, it is vital that teachers ask themselves difficult questions about their practice.

The chapter reflects on the nature of being critical in education and returns to a question outlined in the introduction: is it ever possible to represent the Other as anything else than the Other? This is the time for teachers who are committed to justice to review everything we do, whatever the origin or pedigree and however challenging it is to our own beliefs.

I have tried to reveal the contradictory ways in which Islam is represented in education. While many of the initiatives I have discussed are motivated by a desire to cultivate positive relationships between members of different faiths, they have taken place in the context of a perception of Islam as the antithesis of western liberalism and of a systematic demonisation of Islam. As long as western powers, their media and political bodies define western liberalism as the antidote to the perceived illiberal Islam there can be no unprejudiced representation of Islam, only attempts to negotiate the Other. The relationship between knowledge, power and representation of Islam (as discussed in my introduction) makes it impossible to represent the Other fairly or equitably, because the relationship between the Other and us is neither fair nor equal.

Samir Amin points out that the representation of Islam as a particular type of knowledge is remade and reformulated within each new social context. Each new context entails a new engagement between the West and the Other, the West and Islam (Amin, 2010). Here I argue that the form of engagement taken in contemporary educational practice and theory is through a discourse of tolerance.

In education, the most common representations of Islam are informed by a desire to promote tolerance as a positive value. But as I argue below, it is problematic. In a context in which Islamophobia and strategies of integration provide the ideological backdrop, Islam in education remains subject to the dominant ideas of the Other.

Toledo and the Code of Practice

The way Islam is represented in education seems to be coloured by extremes. At one end of the spectrum we find veiled or explicit references in the media or official strategies like *Contest* and *Prevent* to Islam as a source of terrorism and extremism. At the other end are resources and teaching materials designed to promote positive representation of Islam, which stress the spiritual depths of Islam as well as its contribution to world civilisation, including in the West.

It is the latter representation that is arguably most challenging because it presents itself as pro-Islam or at least as set in a framework that aims to represent all religions equally. Not only do most pedagogies that underlie the teaching of religion in schools aim to foster pupils' appreciation of all religions, but also most teachers assume that one of the main aims of RE is to teach all world religions equally. One of the defining features of RE as a curriculum subject is that teachers, the agreed syllabi and the guidelines identify the equal promotion of all religions as a key aspect of facilitating better understanding towards religious communities. Consequently teachers, and the resources they use, are generally committed to presenting representations of religion which counter negative stereotypes.

The RE Council Code of Practice for teachers of RE exemplifies this approach. It is designed to support teachers who teach RE as they negotiate the challenges posed by teaching pupils of various beliefs about beliefs that are different from their own and beliefs that are controversial. The nine points in the Code of Practice focus on creating a classroom environment that is neutral towards religious and non-religious beliefs. Teachers are encouraged to show respect to all pupils and to 'practice reciprocity' in that they treat the beliefs of others with the same respect 'as they would like their own beliefs to be treated in the same circumstances'. The need for balance is emphasised: teachers should encourage a range of views 'even if they find this uncomfortable on occasion' and should 'promote fair and accurate representation'. The Code warns teachers not to make generalisations or comparisons between religions and recommends that sound scholarship and a range of voices should inform their teaching (REC, 2009).

The tone of the Code of Practice conveys commitment to the equal and fair representation of all religions – as does the tone of the Toledo Guiding Principles. The Organisation for Security and Co-Operation in Europe (OSCE), along with a panel of Experts on Freedom of Religion or Belief, met in Toledo, Spain in 2007 to discuss approaches to the teaching of religion in state schools. The meeting and the intensive consultation process that followed aimed to develop guidelines and criteria for public schools which were teaching about different religions.

The ten guiding principles from Toledo recommend that all teaching about religions should be based on comprehensive knowledge and understanding and an environment that is respectful of human rights. Like the RE Code of Practice for teachers of RE, it stresses the need for objective, fair and balanced representation of all religions. The Toledo guidelines go further than the REC; they recommend that curricula and existing guidelines that are insufficiently objective should be revised and that teachers should be adequately trained in the skills and knowledge to be able to interact with students respectfully and sensitively. Like the REC Code of Practice, the Toledo Guidelines remind teachers that different religions are experienced differently depending on their history and cultural context (OSCE/ODIHR, 2007).

The desire to present religions positively and to recognise diversity is written into the national Non-Statutory Framework for RE (NSFRE) and into most agreed syllabi. The NSFRE begins by stating that RE is important because it encourages children to learn from different religions and beliefs and enables pupils to develop respect and sensitivity to others (QCA, 2004:6). It recommends that students investigate the diversity both between and within religions and the different perceptions in society about the role of religion.

However, the policy and guidelines for RE have to be judged in the context of the current political and educational climate.

Tolerance may be a common aim in education but why is the idea so popular in RE and why is it so ubiquitous (Afdal, 2010)? What does 'tolerance' or 'toleration' mean?. Advocacy of toleration is meaningless and impossible without an apology or a revision of its meaning. Henry Ruf (1997) argues that 'merely' tolerating someone who is different 'seems grossly inadequate' yet he defends the term. Zagorin (2003)

argues that the term has so many negative connotations that it is difficult to see how it ever came to be morally desirable.

Writers who find tolerance an inadequate idea may develop typologies
which attempt to redefine the term so it is more acceptable. Tyler (2008)
is a typical example. He argues that tolerance as a paradigm creates its
binary opposite; in the case of Islam and the West, it is Islam that becomes the 'baneful Other'. He defends the concept on the grounds that
tolerance can be differentiated from 'genuine tolerance'. While tolerance
is judgemental, genuine tolerance is 'judgemental beneficence': it recognises the behaviour of the Other as inferior or even offensive but it
affirms the 'inviolable humanity of the bearer' (Tyler, 2008:160).

Writing about the relationship between education for tolerance and
individualised religion, Friedrich Schweitzer (2007) distinguishes between 'thin' and 'thick' tolerance: thin tolerance is the impersonal rule
that we are supposed to be tolerant, whereas thick tolerance is able to
withstand the test of conflicting convictions.

The most common criticism of tolerance is that it is not only grudging
and ungracious but that it places the tolerated in a subservient position
to the tolerator. The word tolerance is derived from the Latin to *endure*,
and we only tolerate that which we find disagreeable or in some way
alien – we do not tolerate that which we love (Razavi and Ambuel, 1997).
Furthermore, toleration is not a universal or enduring virtue. The unequal nature of the relationship between the tolerated and the tolerator
means that toleration can be withdrawn at any time (Brown, 2006).

If even its supporters feel the need to qualify and justify its use, why is
tolerance so popular? One answer lies in the role it is expected to play
in a diverse society. McClure believes that tolerance has many short-
comings but is a necessary virtue, a practical virtue in modern society,
because it functions to mediate conflict and misunderstanding between the beliefs and values of communities (McClure, 1990).

The necessity of tolerance is rooted in certain relationships and
assumptions. First, where there are different groups or communities
within society, there is the potential for conflict due to the competing
systems of values and truth claims. The second assumption is that
where there is conflict, bigotry or violence because of such differences,

tolerance can act as a mediating discourse. Its usefulness, and therefore its attractiveness to educationalists, is in direct relation to the perceived conflict generated by diverse societies. If we live in a plural society, we need to inculcate tolerance as a virtue. Justifying toleration despite its failings, philosopher Richard Dees explains the relationship between diversity and toleration in the following way:

> Without tolerance, diversity can – and often does – lead to civil war. Undoubtedly, a pluralism that celebrates diversity requires more than tolerance, it requires people to value different cultures and beliefs for their own sake. Groups that merely tolerate each other exist in a cold war. But toleration is a necessary first step. (Dees, 1997:134)

The popularity of tolerance is usually located within the binary of diversity/plurality and conflict. Its desirability is not intrinsic to the concept itself, but lies within its function and use: the alleviation of conflict between groups. The notion is that the existence of different ideas, value systems and customs within the same society generates conflict and that tolerance is the mechanism by which that conflict can be alleviated. It may be a passive virtue and it may not go far enough but, as Mehdi Razavi and David Amuel (1997) argue, tolerance is 'the necessary condition for having a civil society'. The implication is that while tolerance is not a perfect idea, the absence of tolerance in a plural society is far worse.

The conflict/tolerance binary recurs continually, especially in education. Tolerance is advocated in discussions about preventing conflict between groups and communities. It is in the many agreed syllabi that the relationship between the tolerance and the potential conflict generated by diversity is most explicitly articulated. In England the East Sussex Agreed Syllabus opens with the observation that 'our society has never been so diverse' and that good RE has a crucial role in making Britain a country that is tolerant and peaceful (2011). The Ealing Agreed Syllabus of 2008 lists the cultivation of tolerance as the second aim (the first is promotion of self-esteem), explaining that this is particularly important in such a diverse borough (Ealing, 2008).

Many agreed syllabi link the cultivation of tolerance with particular attitudes or approaches to the study of religion. In the Foreword to the review of the Luton Agreed Syllabus, Cllr Tahir Khan stresses that RE is more than just teaching about religion; it is about encouraging certain attitudes towards religion. He points out that RE offers us the chance to teach children from an early age how to tolerate cultural differences (Khan, 2011).

This understanding of tolerance and its role in education is particularly associated with multicultural strategies. Multiculturalism as an approach which acknowledges cultural difference and even celebrates it has, as we saw in Chapter Two, been a feature of RE for some time, to the extent that many in RE see the role of their subject as an arbitrator of difference and of competing claims to truth (Barnes, 2007). In the context of multiculturalism, tolerance facilitates differences. It is concerned with enabling those who live in a society which is not monolithic to negotiate and accommodate difference. In this sense, the many critiques of tolerance that accuse it of not going far enough are almost redundant because even a minimal definition of tolerance will allow different groups to coexist without conflict. In a multicultural context it can be enough that tolerance enables groups to live alongside each other without conflict. Where it is accepted that there are differences and that those differences of culture and values can be accommodated in a plural society, it is enough that tolerance acts as the lubricant that allows the many cultural cogs to turn without friction.

So when Muslim women in England began to wear veils and to dress in ways that are 'unwestern', this excited little hostility even when Islam was subject to such controversies as the Rushdie affair. For the same reason there was little objection to Muslim families and communities living in predominantly Muslim neighbourhoods – they were generally perceived as 'Asian' communities and were not considered a threat to Britishness or English customs. It is to comply with tolerance that most RE textbooks throughout the 1980s and 1990s attempted to represent aspects of Islam neutrally and objectively (see Chapter Three). Differences in customs and beliefs were presented as differences of lifestyle and culture that could be integrated into a broader understanding of what it meant to be British, and the concept of tolerance served to accommodate rather than to pass judgement.

Copley notes that the concept of tolerance was linked to the development of the world-religions approach to the teaching of religions in schools (Copley, 2003). Consequently the practices and beliefs of Islam were represented neutrally – the aim of the lessons was not to engage pupils in critical study of the beliefs and practices in Islam, but to encourage majority groups to tolerate them. John Hull (2000) might argue that true tolerance demands that pupils appreciate the common essence at the heart of all religions, but if the stated aim (as it is the NSFRE and countless agreed syllabi) is to negate hostility and conflict between groups and to equip young people with the attitudes and skills to do this, then the most minimal definition of tolerance is enough.

Tolerance and integration

In *The End of Tolerance* (2007), Arun Kundnani writes about the events, policies and discussions surrounding the growing hostility in the UK towards Muslims and Islam. He describes the escalation in this hostility but situates it in the context of a radical shift in the conceptualisation of racism. He argues that from 2000, the 'concept of racism was turned on its head' (Kundnani, 2007:131). Previously racism was increasingly recognised as an important issue that should be challenged in all institutions including schools. However, as the language of community cohesion emerged, the desire to create a unified national culture became the dominant factor in how racism was understood. Kundnani describes the process:

> It was no longer a question of the ways in which society systematically excluded particular groups and thus set in train a process of ghettoisation. It was supposed instead, that non white groups themselves refused to integrate and this made themselves strange to whites, some of whom then became hostile. (Kundnani, 2007:132)

It was an underlying assumption of the community cohesion agenda that minority groups were themselves to blame for their inability to assimilate. They were responsible for the lack of a national culture. The failure to integrate was identified as the major cause of racial tension and conflict. Muslims were identified as problematic when they exhibited values and customs that appeared to be outside the parameters of British culture. Kundnani refers to this shift as the 'end of tolerance'.

Education is one site where the idea of tolerance still prevails but its meaning and the consequences of its use have changed. The language of tolerance is still a routine part of the rationale and objectives for RE, but where it was once understood as part of a narrative that saw the relationships between religions through a multicultural prism, tolerance is now framed by educational approaches based on community cohesion and integrationist objectives.

The assumption that diversity leads to conflict and that what is needed is integration, and not a plurality of different but mutually respectful groups, limits the level of difference that can be accommodated. Some Muslim practices and beliefs are considered acceptable and may be tolerated, while some are deemed unacceptable and therefore not tolerated. This is apparent in many of the *Prevent* documents but it is also implicit in the way Islam is represented in textbooks and in school pedagogies. Aspects of Islam that are perceived as challenging Western or liberal norms are either omitted from the syllabus or presented in such a way that they are made to resemble western – and therefore tolerable – practices.

The representation of Islam in textbooks does not challenge such views. The rise of Islamism, the fact that Islam is connected with many international conflicts and associated with terrorist groups such as Al-Qaida is rarely addressed. Neither extremism nor conflict fits with Britishness and British values so RE textbooks choose to ignore it. Of the textbooks written for secondary pupils, only one mentions Islamism and only two include sections that discuss Islam as a political or radical force in global politics. That which cannot be tolerated is simply omitted.

Although there is some recognition that RE should engage with issues that are controversial and challenging if its content is to be relevant to pupils (Marshall, 2010), issues to do with terrorism or extremism in Islam are seldom addressed. If issues to do with extremism and Islam are included in RE, they are removed from the main body of the RE curriculum and appear only in the *RE*silience programme. The effective segregation of issues to do with radical Islam or even a politicised Islam in a discrete field reinforces the distinction between aspects of Islam that can be tolerated, so are acceptable and part of the curriculum, and those which are not.

The integrationist drive excludes elements of Islam that cannot be integrated. Tolerance acts as the mechanism by which beliefs or practices are judged. If it is tolerable it can be integrated and considered part of the tapestry that makes up British values and Britishness. If it is judged to go beyond the boundaries of what can be reasonably accepted, it is not tolerable.

Whatever the critics of multiculturalism argue – that multiculturalism essentialised difference or that it encouraged difference over unified identities – they did not isolate difference as inherently problematic. In the context of an integrationist framework, difference must always be regulated before it can be accepted. Tolerance is no longer about mediating relationships between groups, as it was with multiculturalism. It is now about regulating difference. The implication is that while some differences may be accommodated, some are too different and have no place in British society. Accordingly, some aspects of Islam or practices associated with Muslim life are routinely included in education, especially when limited to the cultural, but the aspects which are political or which challenge existing norms must be qualified or omitted.

Understanding the relationship between tolerance and education in this way echoes discussions about the impact of a liberal paradigm in education. The drive to repackage and streamline religious beliefs and practices so they fit a liberal paradigm better means that religions are represented in ways that accommodate a liberal agenda. Tolerance acts as a form of censorship, but an integrationist model creates a further level of regulation. Islam is regulated through the prism of tolerance and then again through the limitations imposed by what it is deemed desirable to integrate.

Both liberal and integrationist frameworks omit representations of certain aspects of Islam. The Islam that appears in the classroom has usually been streamlined: certain beliefs and manifestations are left off the curriculum because they sit uncomfortably with liberal values and expectations. This is a silent process. Most pupils and perhaps teachers are unaware, for instance, that the cultural form of Islam presented in most textbooks is based on an Islam that has its roots in the practices of families originally from Pakistan. When textbooks fail to acknowledge the specific cultural, theological or political contexts of Islam, they are representing a particular form of Islam as a universal type; they are representing through omission.

106

In the case of an integrationist approach, the process of omission is different. Aspects or interpretations of Islam are ignored not because they do not fit a particular interpretation of Islam but because they are judged to be inferior. Political philosopher Wendy Brown describes this process in *Regulating Aversion* (2008), unravelling the underlying assumptions and implications of the modern usage of the term tolerance. Her analysis is rooted in the particular significance of the time after 9/11 when, she says, the political rhetoric of Islam, fundamentalism, culture and civilisation reframed the discussion of tolerance to legitimise new forms of state action.

Brown's main argument is that tolerance has become a civilising discourse through the culturalisation of difference. All difference, whether political, moral or religious, is reconceptualised as a meeting of cultures. This differs from the scenario presented through multiculturalism, which takes the view that all cultures are equal, only different or, more cynically, that the culture of the west is the first among equals. The culturalisation of politics, according to Brown, 'organises the players'. The translation of Islam, or beliefs and practices associated with Islam, or the customs and forms of government, political histories, philosophies and theologies of Islam become 'cultures', while those of the West are not a culture but part of civilisation (Brown, 2008).

We can see this in the way particular areas of Islam are presented in education. Take, for example, the status of women in Muslim countries or Muslim communities. Textbooks that include sections on women generally talk about the political and social position of women. Although aspects of the way Muslim women dress, their relationships with men and wider society are sometimes determined by religious principles, their status and position in society as women is not reducible to Islam. There may be other factors that shape the way Muslim women look or behave that are not religious (Murti, 2008). Other factors are always at play, yet the issue of 'women in Islam' is presented as an aspect of Muslim culture and religious practice rather than as a political or social or economic issue. Some textbooks on religions other than Islam do have sections on women but it is only in books on Muslims that the position of women is persistently isolated as a particular issue. Not only does this consign Muslim women to the category of a special case, but their lives are characterised by issues that relate to culture rather than to rights or equality. Culture is what non-liberal people are imagined to be ruled and ordered by; liberal people are considered to have culture or cultures (Brown, 2008).

Panjwani (2012) reviewed the books and resources used to teach Islam in schools and found a tendency to present Islam purely as a religion. All facets of Muslim societies are represented through a religious lens, and are thus interpreted as aspects of religiosity and as rooted in religious values and truths. The possibility that Muslim societies may be influenced by factors other than religion is ignored. The single-minded nature of this representation is important because it contrasts strongly with the way aspects of Western society would be understood. Muslims are not accorded the diversity of beliefs and practices, the complex negotiations that individuals who are Christian or who live in Western societies make between their religion and their secular lives. All Muslim life is represented through a single religious lens.

Tolerance, Islam and pedagogy

It is customary to situate the teaching of RE in the desire to promote peace and understanding between groups. Many RE specialists would go so far as to argue that learning about religions and developing the skills needed to understand the spiritual lives of others develops the inner life of pupils and helps them to engage meaningfully with the beliefs and customs of their neighbours (Jackson, 2011). Most teachers believe that the cultivation of tolerance entails encouraging pupils to understand Islam positively. Smalley (2005) argues that pupils should be made aware of the normality of Muslim family life, so as to counter negative stereotypes and foster understanding that Muslim families share the same preoccupations – such as meals, family occasions and celebrations – as everyone else.

However this desire to emphasise the positive is rooted in assumptions about the nature of Islam that are as problematic as those articulated in the *Contest* documents. Due to the regulatory function of tolerance, schools and the state assume the role of neutral arbiters in deciding what is taught and how. The assumption on which recent policies from the Home Office are predicated is that there is an acceptable Islam that can be integrated and an unacceptable Islam that should be excluded. This distinction separates the Islam that is taught as part of the normal curriculum from the Islam that is taught as part of *RE*silience. The assumption that only the acceptable Islam should be represented in education is evident in the invisible Islam that is often missing from discussions, textbooks and resources.

Many discussions about teaching Islam begin with the recognition that after 9/11 the climate of racism and hostility against Muslims intensified (Jackson, 2011). Teachers and specialists have responded differently depending on how they understand the role of education in relation to Islam. Some believe it is more important than ever to emphasise the common bonds between Islam, Christianity and Judaism as a way of countering hostility towards Muslims. Others are keen to stress that terrorism and extremism are only ever the actions of a minority and may not even be considered a legitimate expression of Islam (Smalley, 2005). These approaches have in common a belief in tolerance as a positive virtue in teaching about Islam. They are premised on the belief that while pupils can be encouraged to discuss 'real' Islam, no discussion of the unacceptable face of Islam can be allowed unless it is first defined as unacceptable. Many pedagogies of RE regard tolerance as positive – but the object of tolerance has already been decided. Pupils are encouraged to be tolerant towards people who have different values or beliefs to their own, but only as long as those values or beliefs already fall within the remit of what is deemed tolerable.

Tolerance establishes the boundaries for what may be discussed and how it may be discussed. This is ironic because RE has long been seen as a space where pupils can be encouraged to explore their ideas and opinions, and tolerance constrains any discussion of, or engagement with, Islam. Underlying many models of education for tolerance is the belief that it requires dialogue between the parties, dialogue that is thought to generate the understanding that can lead to empathy and acceptance. However, the dialogue that John Hull and others advocate as part of the process that leads to tolerance is premised on it being a dialogue between equals. For Hull (2000), tolerance is about the recognition of a common essence between communities and individuals. Tolerance as part of the discourse described by Wendy Brown is a relationship between unequal partners. The subject who tolerates and the subject who is tolerated are not equal. The tolerator is in a position of power: they may withdraw their tolerance at any time, and they may

109

demand that the tolerated adjust their actions if they are to continue to be tolerated and must demonstrate their worthiness to be tolerated.

The unequal relationship was explicitly played out through the community cohesion agenda, when Muslim groups were required to demonstrate that they were eligible for funding. The new *Prevent* strategy was partly based on the assumption that too many Muslim groups which did not clearly enough support the values embedded in *Prevent* had received funding. Dame Pauline Neville-Jones, a former security minister, told the BBC in 2011 that 'it was not right for the government to actively assist and advocate those who are advocating quite different values' (Travis, 2011).

In education and especially RE, community cohesion is presented as a strategy designed to alleviate tensions and promote understanding between groups. However, the assumptions underpinning community cohesion in wider society remains true within education. It is still the case that the notion of community is precisely defined so that only those communities that are acceptable are included in the strategy. It is hard to see how there can be equal dialogue between groups when the nature and extent of that dialogue is still decided by only one partner in the community cohesion relationship.

Tolerance acts to inhibit engagement in the classroom in yet another way. Tolerance has become not only the strategy that informs how Islam is taught but also the endpoint. This perspective resembles that offered by Barnes and Panjwani in their respective analyses of the consequences of the liberal paradigm in the teaching of religion. Both authors note that the concern to promote a liberal interpretation of religion means that only some forms of religion are represented and then only in specific contexts. To understand how the elevation of tolerance as a key educational aim in reality undermines engagement, we need to consider the context in which these associations take place.

In the UK, Islam and Muslims are routinely associated with terrorism and extremism, and Muslim practices are commonly perceived as anti-western. Only some aspects or interpretations of Islam are accepted as worthy of tolerance. Islam must be represented in such a way that it fits the ideal of the 'good' Islam described in the *Contest* and *Prevent* documents. As we saw in Chapter Four, this Islam is apolitical, its adherents are part of the democratic process and its practices and beliefs are founded on acceptable values that allow them to be integrated into British society. It is the creation of an essentially compliant Islam, an Islam that has adapted and conformed to Britishness. The combination of a climate hostile to Muslims, plus the drive to represent an Islam that can be tolerated, largely determines the nature of curriculum Islam and the pedagogies employed.

That only an idealised and compliant Islam is promoted through the curriculum distorts the focus of lessons on Islam. If the end result of the lesson is that students engage with an Islam that is tolerable, then lessons are no longer about Islam but about tolerance. The focus of lessons is not to engage with Islam but to learn the importance of tolerance and how to tolerate Islam. The teaching of Islam (or any religion) becomes the means by which we teach tolerance. The connection between RE and the promotion of tolerance as an educational objective is, as I have argued, close. In the agreed syllabi, RE is especially described as a means by which tolerance can be cultivated.

There are two ironies here. RE has gained especial justification for its role as the arbiter of tolerance in the curriculum precisely because Islam is associated with intolerance. Secondly, through the representation of an idealised, depoliticised Islam young people are actually less well prepared to negotiate the barrage of anti-Islamic images and associations that are rife in the media and popular discourse. Curriculum Islam, with its emphasis on the Five Pillars, its stylised representation of history and its collapse of the enormous cultural, denominational and national diversity of Muslim life into a single ideal Islam prepares pupils for an Islam that does not exist. If the aim of education about Islam really is to encourage pupils to show tolerance, it would surely be more useful if they could engage with a form of Islam that relates to what they learn about it outside the classroom rather than an idealised stereotype.

Question everything

In a book that argues that Islam has been misrepresented through education it would be gratifying if I could propose a perfect model of representation, and were able to hold it up and say 'this is what Islam really looks like'. So how should Islam be represented? And should the representation of Islam in education be different from the way Islam is portrayed in other disciplines? Should young children be 'protected' from aspects of the debates about Islam that are controversial or contentious? Questions of how Islam should be represented in education presume that that there is a single undisputed answer to each one, waiting just beyond the grasp of educationalists, to be discovered and implemented in the curriculum and enshrined in textbooks.

Teachers who seek a representation of Islam often look towards Muslim communities to provide the definitive answer to their questions. In his essay on teaching Islam in schools, Michele Bertani (2004) describes how teachers take children on trips to mosques or arrange for representatives from local Muslim communities to visit schools and talk about their religion. To Lynn Davies (2008) these strategies are 'simplistic' because they avoid the far more complex question of whether any individual or mosque can truly represent Islam. She compares the assumption that a visit to the local Islamic community centre would be useful with an imagined school visit to the house of a humanist where pupils could 'marvel at the ritual consumption of alcohol. See how we are in veneration in harmony in front of old reruns of Friends. Look carefully at the preservation of the sacred dust balls under the bed...' (Davies, 2008:86). Davies maintains that it is simply not possible to use isolated, decontextualised examples of religious practice to represent people's beliefs.

Emphasising the differences and the culturally located nature of Islam does not answer the question of how Islam should be represented in the classroom. Not only does it make the question of representation nonsensical but it is also problematic. Andrew Wright (2007) argues that the theory that there is no essence to a religion, that there is no eternal core of belief or mystery that is true for that religion wherever and whenever it is located, means that we avoid the question of the unique core of a religion. Pedagogies that avoid engaging with the fact that some religions embrace a universal claim to truth are representing those religions selectively. He believes that since absolute truth claims are a part of many religious traditions, to avoid the question of truth claims is itself a form of misrepresentation (Wright, 2007).

Tariq Modood makes a similar point in his discussion of the way we recognise religious groups. He believes that what he terms radical anti-essentialism 'is inherently destructive'. This is a process where each identity – Muslim, black women, immigrant etc – is shown to be illusory because ultimately all can be broken down into the experiences of each individual. Modood argues that this would mean that there was no Islam. This is problematic for those who do believe that there is a shared Islam because it renders all groups 'mythic and dishonest unities'. He argues that it is possible to identify what he terms as 'continuity' in cultures, rather than essentialism (Modood, 1998). So just as it is possible to identify a continuity between the language of Shakespeare, Dickens and Rushdie, it is possible to identify the continuity between the Islam of Pakistan, the Islam of Morocco, the Islam of France or of Saudi Arabia.

Modood's observation nonetheless leaves many questions for education unanswered. For a start, how would such a 'continuity' be determined? Traditionally, the strategy has been to invite Muslims to participate in writing school textbooks and joining SACREs, the local bodies that decide what and how religions should be taught in schools. But merely considering how Islam should be represented fails to address the larger question of why Islam is represented in the way it is and the consequences for pupil learning about Islam through current practice.

The way we engage with Islam and religions more generally is problematic, as reflected in the wide-ranging debates. The nature of dialogue with and between religious traditions (Barnes, 2002), the differences between comparing religions as opposed to encountering religions (Schweitzer, 2009), the advantages of pedagogies that stress intercultural education or education for peace, are all attempts by educationalists to work towards a way of engaging with religions that embody differences not just of belief but of culture, ethnicity and values.

In their analysis of the debates around race, multiculturalism and culture, Blommaert and Verschueren (1998) describe the discourse as omnipresent. But they point out that at the core of all these strategies is the assumption that difference is problematic. The idea that difference needs to be packaged underpins education for tolerance. They note that the very attempt to negotiate difference, to make it acceptable, to celebrate it or make it palatable to the next generation, is really nothing more than the assumption that the normal state of affairs is homogeneity and uniformity.

Tariq Ramadan (2010) argues that there has never been more talk of diversity and plurality yet that we seem to be trapped by these differences. Despite the endless talk of plurality and difference, however positive it may be, we seem to understand each other less; if we are a global village, it is a village full of villagers who know nothing about each other. The problem for many educationalists is that any negotiation of difference is problematic because in the West, the recognition of difference as a primary marker is the recognition of the Other. This tension is vividly illustrated through the representation of Islam in the curriculum. Were Muslims treated fairly in the West, were international relations not based on the perception of Islam as a threat to democracy, were there no inequalities of opportunity in education or employment on grounds of race or ethnicity or religion, then we could refer to difference merely as a descriptive category. But if Ramadan is right and the focused gaze on diversity brings not clarity but only greater difference, and if the burden of the Other compromises the very attempt to represent Islam, we must ask whether accurate representation is even possible.

The role of dialogue in challenging misrepresentation is recognised as important. This desire to facilitate dialogue as a positive tool in the way people engage with difference drives REDCo (religion, education, dialogue, conflict), a project designed to investigate educational strategies to 'recognise each other and to learn from each other, rather than to perpetuate divisions' (Weisse, 2011:6). REDCo is an enormously ambitious venture that looks at the potential relationship between the nature of religious education and the way young people understand difference. The research methodologies and rationale of REDCo are based on an interpretative approach to RE that was originally developed for use in state schools in England and Wales. The interpretative approach rejects the idea that students should be inducted into a particular world-view or particular epistemological stance. It aims to 'help children and young people to find their own positions within the key debates about religious plurality' and has a radical and critical centre (Jackson, 2004:87). The strands to REDCo include: challenging conventional models of religions as fixed and homogeneous, interpreting and engaging with religious phenomena rather than the distancing more commonly associated with phenomenological approaches and, lastly, reflexivity.

Robert Jackson (2011) describes the different strands of reflexivity but the one I am most interested in here is the requirement for the learner or researcher to be critical. The word 'critical' crops up frequently in discussions on education. There are critical pedagogies, there is critical thinking, critical theory and the development of criticality. The meaning of words that are used frequently and freely is often lost and becomes contested but I suggest that, despite the ubiquitous use of the term 'critical', it retains a radical core that would allow us to approach the issue of the representation of Islam from a new and useful direction. Criticality demands that the subject under scrutiny be actively engaged.

Being critical is not just about asking questions, even challenging questions; it is about asking questions that expose relationships of power and dominance (Carr and Kemmis, 1986). And the inquiry itself is not about those relationships as they relate to the self but as they relate to issues of justice and social freedom. Being critical is driven not by the desire for self-emancipation but by a desire for social equality (Carr, 1998). Its starting point is not the self but the attempt to address inequality and injustice. Being critical is situated in a particular context – it is not an abstract skill that can be transferred from one part of the curriculum to another. The force and impact of criticality is the specificity of its focus (Winch, 2005).

Criticality, then, is not an attitude but a relationship between the subject and the environment. The precursor to criticality is the enquirer, the reflective subject who is willing to question. Habermas (1970) called this act of criticality the experience of reflection, the capacity and the will to seek rational self-determination. Being critical demands that we be prepared to expose unequal relationships, to situate ourselves against existing models of authority and to question the *status quo*. Friere reinforces Habermas's position, saying that the 'integrated person is person as subject' (Friere, 2005:4). Friere's integrated person refuses to accept existing power relationships and transcends the social and political relationships that usually bind us and, most importantly, gives this position voice.

So what might a critical approach to Islam in education look like? The OSCE/ODIHR – the organisations which developed the Toledo principles for teaching religions – recently published a report about challenging discrimination against Muslims in education. This report, *Guidelines for Educators on Countering Intolerance and Discrimination against Muslims*, recommends that teachers develop and 'implement learning activities that proactively encourage critical thinking and reflection' (OSCE/ODIHR, 2011:34). The report suggests strategies for doing this, such as discussion, case studies, role play and a range of creative activities. It recognises that a critical approach must take into account the experiences of Muslims and the legitimacy of the issues and concerns of Muslim.

Being critical and attempting to represent the Other are contradictory aims. If they are to be the subjects, the subjects must speak themselves. If we outsiders represent Islam, however benignly, we are already imposing limits on what is permissible or acceptable. If we wish to act as integrated persons we must be prepared first to question every way we have represented Islam so far and acknowledge that there has been no disinterested engagement with Islam. In his critique of the teaching of black history in American schools, Joe Kincheloe finds it unacceptable that the subject be taught without a 'critical edge'. He describes a form of education that is 'so acontextual, so devoid of conflict' that the reality of 'the American black experience is concealed' (Kincheloe, 1993). Being critical in relation to Islam in education entails bringing students and pupils to the experience of Muslim lives in all their contexts. In the UK that involves bringing pupils to inequalities, discrimination, racism and Islamophobia as well as the theological, spiritual and communal aspects of Islam.

Being critical also demands that we turn our gaze not to Islam itself but to our own assumptions and practices. The state plays a significant role in creating the contexts in which the representations of Islam occur. It is not aloof from the relationships that create and perpetuate Islamophobia but is an integral part of the process. In *The End of Tolerance* (2007) Arun Kundnani argues that the state is responsible for the hostility and discrimination that has emerged towards Muslims (Kundnani, 2007). Shiraz Thobani has identified a similar pattern in education. He argues that the state is responsible for the cultivation of a diminished and impoverished curriculum on Islam (Thobani, 2010). The curriculum is controlled by the state through a wide variety of means and teachers are often compelled to tailor their pedagogies and knowledge content to the latest strategy, guidance or policy. A critical approach to Islam in the curriculum requires educationalists to challenge the role of the state in the creation of Islamophobia and curriculum Islam. It would demand that, at the very least, ideas about community cohesion or the question of whether it is legitimate that the Home Office *Prevent* agenda inform the teaching of Islam would be constantly debated by teachers and specialists.

Criticality must have consequences (Clegg, 2005): we must close the gap between critique and practice. The current climate allows Muslim communities to be publically berated for failing to integrate, for insisting on living in Muslim communities, or for not fitting into a version of Britishness determined by the coalition government. This is justification enough for us to review the way we approach Islam in schools.

Books which claim to present Islam as a religion of peace but which fail to deal with the factors that discriminate against Muslims at home and abroad are unacceptable. The curriculum similarly requires critical attention. Critical approaches to education are daunting because they are challenging or confrontational and the task can seem too large for a single person to make a difference. But because teachers engage with policy and the interpretation of policy every day, they have more opportunities than most to engage critically with pupils and students. They now find themselves in a political double bind: they must have due regard to the Equality Act, yet undermining fundamental British values counts as unprofessional conduct.

Accordingly, teachers have to question the legitimacy of British values as the benchmark for the values of all communities. The origins and the implications of the obligation in *Prevent* to teach Britishness could be exposed in classroom discussions and in the training of teachers. The factors that distort our perception of Muslims could be challenged by adopting a critical approach to the representation of Islam in education. And a new representation of Islam, drawn not by government or the media but by those who are represented, should be evolved and adopted in education and wider society. The voices and experiences of

117

Muslims, the role of the state and awareness of the nature and impact of Orientalism must all inform the representation of Muslim lives. Only then can Islam be taught appropriately in schools.

Books Discussed

Abdullah, N (2000) *What do we say (A Guide to Islamic Manners)*. Leicester: The Islamic Foundation

Amini, I (1995) *The Children's Book on Islam*. Tehran: International Publishing Co

Arnold, E (1981) *Islamic Belief and Practice*. London: Edward Arnold

Baghgat, A (1983) *The Whale of Jonah*. London: Shorouk

Bartlett, C (2009) *AQA A GCSE Islam Religious Studies*. Cheltenham: Nelson Thornes

Blaylock, L (ed) (2004) *Representing Religions*. Birmingham: Christian Education Publishers

Boyce, R (1972) *The Story of Islam*. Exeter: The Religious Education Press

Brown, E (1997) *Religious Education for All*. London: David Fulton

Bruce, R (1984) *Muhammad*. Eastbourne: Holt, Rinehart and Winston

Butler, S (2009) *Religion and Morality AQA (B) GCSE*. Oxfordshire: Philip Allan

Campbell, J and Patrick, S (2010) *GCSE Citizenship Studies for AQA*. Oxford: Heinemann

Chaudhry, R (1991) *Ahmad and Sarah go to the Mosque*. Surrey: Islam International Publications

Chaudhry, R (1983) *Muslim Festivals and Ceremonies*. Tilford: Islam International Publications

Craigen, G and White, J (2006) *Believing and Living – A Text for the WEJEC GCSE Short Course*. London: Hodder and Stoughton

Culshaw, C and Clarke (2006) *Citizenship Today*. London: Collins

Denffer, A (2010) *Islam for Children*. Leicester: The Islamic Foundation

Donohoe, H (2004) *Terrorism*. London: Franklin Watts

Draycott, P (ed) (2007) *Interfaith RE*. Birmingham: Christian Education Publishers

Edmonds, I (1977) *Islam*. London: Franklin Watts

Elais, J (1999) *Islam*. London: Routledge

Friedenthal, L and Kavanah, D (2007) Religions of Africa. Philadelphia: Mason Crest Publishers

Ganeri, A (2003) The Qur'an and Islam. London: Evans Brothers

Ganeri, A (2001) *Islamic Stories*. London: Evans Brothers

Ghani, A (2004) *I can Pray Anywhere*. Leicester: The Islamic Foundation

Green, J and J Mayled (2009) *Islam GCSE Religious Studies for OCR A*. London: Hodder Education

Hands, K and Smith, P (2009) *Religious Studies A Islam: Ethics*. Cheltenham: Nelson Thornes

Harrison, S and Shepard, D (1980) *A Muslim Family in Britain*. Exeter: Religious Education Press

Hartney, C (2004) *Islam*. Cambridge: Cambridge University Press

Hassan, F. Tomlinson, R and Wood C (2009) *Religious Studies A, Islam* (OCR GCSE) Essex: Heinemann.

Hayden, D (2009) *Religious Studies A Islam*. Cheltenham: Nelson Thornes

Holden – Rowley, T and Blewitt, J (2009) *AS Citizenship*. London: Hodder and Stoughton

Hulton (1983) *Islam*. London: Hulton Educational Publications

Husain, M (2006) *Islam and the Global World*. Dubuque: McGraw Hill

Iqbal, M and, Iqbal, M (1976) *Understanding Your Muslim Neighbour*. Cambridge: Lutterworth Press

Kassamali, T. (1996) *The Holy Prophet*. Richmond: Tayyiba Publishers and Distributors

Keene, M and Keene, J (1997) *Junior Steps in RE*. Cheltenham: Stanley Thornes

Kerven, R (1998) *Ramadan and Id-Ul-Fitr*. London: Evans Brothers Ltd

Khan, S (2011) *My First Quran*. New Delhi: Goodword

Knight, K (2010) *My Muslim Faith*. London: Evans Brothers

Le Pla, F and Richards, C (1996) *Islam: Teacher's Resource Book (Living Religions)*. London: Nelson Thornes

Luxenburg, A (2010) *Radical Islam*. Philadelphia: Mason Crest Publishers

Lynch, M (1990) *Islam – A Pictorial Guide*. Derby: Christian Education Movement

Lynch, S, Clinton, C and Orchard, J (2005) *Islam in Todays World*. London: Hodder Murray

Macdonald, F (1991) The World of Islam up to the 1500s. London: Collins Educational

Mantin, P and Mantin R (1993) *The Islamic World: beliefs and civilisations 600-1600*. Cambridge: Cambridge University Press

Maqsood, R (1995) *Islam*. Essex: Heinemann

Maqsood, R (2004) *GCSE Islam The Do – It – Yourself – Guide*. London: Islamic Vision

Marchant, K (1996) *Id-Il-Fitr*. London: Wayland

Mayled, J (2007) *Christianity and Islam*. Cheltenham: Nelson Thornes

Meade, F and Zimmermann, A. (1966) *Religions of the World*. Edinburgh: Holmes McDougall Ltd

Nazir, A (1984) *I am a Muslim*. London: Franklin Watts

Parry, L and Hayes, J (2009) *Religion and Morality GCSE Religious Studies for AQA B*. London: Hodder Education

Protheroe, R and Meherali, R(1984) *Visiting a Mosque*. London: Luetterworth Educational

Quinlivan, V (1984) *Spotlight on Islam*. London: Cassell

Radcliffe, B (2003) *Britain A Diverse Society*. London: PfP Publishing

Read, G and Rudge, J (1994) *Muslims 1*. Birmingham: Westhill RE Centre

Reid, G and Tyler, S (2009) *Religion and Life (Christianity and Islam)*. Essex: Pearson Education Ltd

Rose, D (2007) *Folens Photopack Islam*. Bedfordshire: Folens

Sardar, F (1997) *The Food We Eat*. Leicester: The Islamic Foundation

Sarwar, G (1981) *Islam for Younger People*. Leicester: Muslim Educational Trust

Shilson – Thomas, A (1996) *Stories from World Religions*. Harmondsworth: Puffin

Spradberry, D (2009) *Religion and Life Islam*. Essex: Pearson Education Ltd

Stent, D (1984) *Religious Studies O Level and CSE*. London: Letts Key Facts Books

Stone, S (1988) *Eid ul-Fitr*. London: A&C Black

Tames, R (1982) *Approaches to Islam. London: John Murray*

Taylor, I (2009) *Religion and Life – Christianity and Islam*. Oxford: Oxford University Press

Taylor, I (2009) *Religion and Society – Christianity and Islam*. Oxford: Oxford University Press

Teichmann, I (2002) *Immigration and Asylum*. London: Franklin Watts

Thompson, J (2005) *Islam A New Approach*. London: Hodder Murray

Thorely, S (1983) *Islam in words and pictures*. Exeter: Religious and Moral Education Press

Tyler, S and Reid, G (2009) *Religion and Life (Christianity and Islam)* Oxfordshire: Philip Allan

Wallace, H (2006) *Islam – Budi's Story*. Kent: Baron's

Watton, V (2009) *Religion and Life (Christianity and Islam)*. London: Hodder Education

Watton, V (2011) *Islam Bullet Guide*. London: Hodder Education

Weston, D and Orchard, J (2009) *Islam in today's world*. London: Hodder Murray

Williams, B (2002) *GCSE Citizenship Studies: Student Book*. Buckingham: Folens

Zuker, J (2005) *Sweet Dates to Eat*. London: Francis Lincoln

References

Abbas, T (2011) *Islamic Radicalism and Multicultural Policies: The British Experience* London: Routledge

Abdel-Fattah, R (2006) *Does my head look big in this?* London: Marion Lloyd Books

Afdal, G (2010) The Maze of Tolerance. In K. Engebreton, M. de Souza, G. Durka, L. Gearon (eds) *International Handbook of Inter-religious Education 4*. London: Springer

Alibhai-Brown, Y (2001) After Multiculturalism. *The Political Quarterly*. 72 (1) p47-56

Allen, C (2010) Islamophobia: From K. I. S. S. To R. I. P. In Sayyid, S. and A. Vakil (eds) *Thinking Through Islamophobia*. London: Hurst and Company

Ameli, R and Marandi, S (2007) *British Muslims' Expectations of the Government.* Wembley: Islamic Human Rights Commission

Amin, S (2010) *Eurocentrism*. London: Monthly Review Press

Arthur, J Gearon, L and Sears, A (2010) *Education, Politics and Religion*. Oxford: Routledge

Asad, T (1990) Multiculturalism and British Identity in the Wake of the Rushdie Affair. *Politics and Society*. 18 (4) p455-480

Badham, P (1989) *Religion, state and society in modern Britain*. London: Edwin Mellen Press

Barnes, L P (2007) Developing a new post-liberal paradigm for British Religious Education. *Journal Belief and Values* 28 (1) p17-32

Barnes, M (2002) *Theology and the Dialogue of Religions*. Cambridge: Cambridge Press

Bartlett, J and Birdwell, J (2010) The Edge of Violence a radical approach to extremism. Available at http://www.demos.co.uk/publications/theedgeofviolence Accessed January 2011

Bates, D (1984) Harold Loukes: Christian Educationalist 1912-1980. *British Journal of Religious Education*. 6 (2) p75-81

Bates, D (1994) Christianity, culture and other religions (Part 1): the origins of the study of world religions in English education. *British Journal of Religious Education*. 17 (1) p5-18

Bates, D (1996) Christianity, culture and other religions (Part 2): F H Hilliard, Ninian Smart and the 1988 Education Reform Act. *British Journal of Religious Education*. 18 (2) p85-102

Bertani, M (2004) Muslims in Italy: social changes and educational practices. In B. van Driel (ed) *Confronting Islamophobia in Practice*. Stoke-on-Trent: Trentham

Bhat, A, Carr-Hill, R and Ohri, S. (1990) *Britain's Black Population*. Hampshire: Arena

Blair, T (2006) Available http://news.bbc.co.uk/1/hi/uk_politics6219626. Accessed December 2011

Blommaert, J and Verschueren, J (1998) *Debating Diversity*. London: Routledge

Bolton, A (1993) An approach to world religions through beliefs and values in years 10 and 11 in a Leicestershire upper school. In C. Erricker, A. Brown and M. Hayward (eds) *Teaching World Religions*. London: Heinemann Educational Publishers

Brandt, G (1986) *The Realization of Anti-Racist Teaching*. Lewes: Falmer Press

Branigan, T (2005) British-born nationals could lose citizenship in bills sanctions *Guardian* 2 December available at www.guardian.co.uk/2005/dec/02/ Accessed June 2011

Bristol, Bath and North East Somerset Agreed Syllabus (2011) http://amv.somerset.gov.uk/

Brown, W (2008) *Regulating Aversion*. Oxford: Princeton Press

Bunglawala (2002) British Muslims and the Media, in *Quest for Sanity: Reflections on September 11 and the Aftermarth*. London: MCB

Bunting, M (2011) Nigella Lawson and the great Burkini cover-up. Available at http/guardian.co.uk/lifeandstyle12011/apr/23/nigella-lawson-bukini-bikini-swimming

Burnett, J (2004) Community Cohesion and the State. *Race and Class*. 45 (3) p1-18

Cameron, D (2007) Speech at Cambridge Interfaith Programme 17 July 2007 available at

Cameron, D (2011) http://www.bbc.co.uk/news/uk-politics-12371994 Accessed November 2011 http://sms.cam.ac.uk/collection/14;jsessionid

Cameron, J (1882) Mahommedanism. In St Giles Lectures. *Faiths of the World*. London: William Blackwood and Sons Limited

Cantle, T (2008) *Community Cohesion*. Hampshire: PalgraveMacmillan

Carpenter, J (1913) *Comparative Religion*. London: Thornton Butterworth Ltd

Carr, W (1998) *For Education*. Buckingham: Open University Press

Carr, W and Kemmis, S (1986) *Becoming Critical: Education, Knowledge and Action Research*. London: Routledge

Clegg, S (2005) Evidence-based practice in educational research: a critical realist critique of systematic review. *British Journal of Sociology of Education* 26 (3) p415-428

Cole, M. (2005) Empires old and new: a Marxist analysis of the teaching of imperialism, actual and potential, in the British school curriculum. In J. Satterthwaite and E. Atkinson (eds) *Discourses of Education in the New Imperialism*. Stoke-on-Trent: Trentham Books

Cole, M (2012) Racism and Education: from Empire to ConDem. In M. Cole (ed) *Education, Equality and Human Rights*. London: Routledge

Commission on Integration and Cohesion: (2007) *Our Shared Future*, Weatherby: CIC

Conroy, J (2011) Does Religious Education Work? A three year investigation into the practices and outcomes of religious education: A Briefing Paper. Available at http://www.gla.ac.uk/schools/education/research//currentreserachprojects/doesreligiouseducationwork/

Copley, T (2003) *Teaching Religion: Fifty Years of Religious Education in England and Wales*. Exeter: University of Exeter Press

Copley, T (2005) *Indoctrination, education and God*. London: SPCK

Cox, E (1966) *Changing Aims in Religious Education*. London: Routledge and Kegan Paul

Davie, G (2007) *The Sociology of Religion*. London: Sage Publications

Davies, L (2008) *Educating Against Extremism*. Stoke on Trent: Trentham

DCSF (2007) *Guidance on the duty to promote community cohesion*. Nottingham: DCSF

DCSF, (2008) Learning Together To be Safe. Available at https://www.education.gov.uk/publications/standard/_arc_SOP/Page11/DCSF-00804-2008

DCSF (2010) Materials used to Teach about World Religions in Schools in England. Report RR197

Dees, R (1997) The Justification of Toleration. In M. Razavi and D. Ambuel (eds) *Philosophy, Religion, and the Question of Intolerance*. Albany: State University of New York Press

Department for Communities in Local Government (2007) *What works in community cohesion*. London: DCLG

Devon, Plymouth and Torbay Agreed Syllabus, 2007. Available at http//:www.devonlpd.orgview_folder.asp?folderid=1051

DES (1971) The Education of Immigrants, *Education Survey* 13. London: HMSO

DES (1977) *Education in Schools: A Consultative Document*. London: HMSO

DES (1985) *Education for All* (The Swann Report). London: HMSO.

DfE (2011) *Teachers' Standards*. Available at http://media.education.gov.uk

DfES (2001) *Guidance after the events of September 11th*. London: HMSO

DfES (2007) *Curriculum Review: Diversity and Citizenship*. Nottingham: DfES

Donnan, H and Stokes, M (2002) Interpreting Interpretations of Islam. In H. Donnan. (ed) *Interpreting Islam*. London: SAGE Publications

Douglass, S and Dunn, R (2002) Interpreting Islam in American Schools. In H. Donnan (ed) *Interpreting Islam*. London: Sage

Ealing Agreed Syllabus, The Marriage of Heaven and Earth; Religious Education for the 21st Century (2007) https://www.egfl.org.uk/categories/teaching

East Sussex Agreed Syllabus (2005) Responding to Religions and Life. Available at http://www.eastsussex.gov.uk. Accessed November 2010

Endres, B (2002) Transcending and attending to difference in the multicultural classroom. *Journal of Philosophy of Education*. 36 (2) p171-185

Falah, G (2005) The visual representation of Muslim/Arab women in daily newspapers in the United States. In G. Falah and C. Nagel (eds) *Geographies of Muslim women: gender, religion, and space*. New York: Guilford Press

Fekete, L (2009) *A Suitable Enemy*. London: Pluto Press

Flint, J and Robinson, D. (eds) (2008) *Community Cohesion in Crisis*. Bristol: Polity Press

Freire, P (2005) *Education for Critical Consciousness*. London: Continuum

Gateway 1.4 Why do People have different beliefs? Available at http://www.re-silience.org.uk/indexphp/en/materials

Gateway 2.1 and 2.4 Demonstrating Respect for Cultures and Religions Adopting An Impartial Stance While Teaching. Available at http://www.re-silience.org.uk/indexphp/en/materials

Gateway 2.2 Displaying Sensitivity to the Home Backgrounds and the Beliefs of Pupils. Available at http://www.re-silience.org.uk/indexphp/en/materials

Gateway 4.3c Religion and Conflict: Partition and its Aftermath. Available at http://www.re-silience.org.uk/indexphp/en/materials

Gateway 4.4 Race Hatred, Especially When Given A Religious Justification. Available at http://.re-silience.org.uk/indexphp/en/materials

Gateway 4.9 Women, Gender Equality and Religion. Available at http://www.re-silience. org.uk/indexphp/en/materials

Gearon, L (2010) Which community? Whose cohesion? Community cohesion, Citizenship and Religious Education: From revolutionary democracy to liberal autocracy. In M. Grimmitt (ed) *Religious Education and Social and Community Cohesion.* Essex: McCrimmons

Gillborn, D (1995) *Racism and Antracism in Real Schools: Theory, Policy, Practice.* Buckingham: Open University Press

Gillborn, D (2008) *Racism and Education.* London: Routledge

Goldman, R (1968) *Readiness for religion: a basis for developmental religious education.* London: Routledge and Kegan Paul

Greaves, R (1998) The borders between religions: A challenge to the world religions approach to religious education. *British Journal of Religious Education* vol. 21 no. 1 20-31

Greaves, R (2005) *Aspects of Islam.* London: Darton Longman and Todd

Grimmitt, M (2000) Introduction: The Captivity and Liberation of Religious Education and the Meaning and Significance of Pedagogy', in Grimmitt, M (ed) *Pedagogies of Religious Education: Case Studies in the Research and Development of Good Pedagogic Practice in RE,* Great Wakering, McCrimmons

Grimmitt, M (2010) Contributing to social and community cohesion. In M. Grimmitt (ed) *Religious Education and Social and Community Cohesion.* Essex: McCrimmons

Habermas, J (1970) Technology and Science as 'Ideology.' In *Toward a Rational Society: Student Protest, Science, and Politics,* trans. Jeremy J. Shapiro. Boston: Beacon Press

Halliday, F (1995) 'Islam is in danger': Rushdie and the struggle for the migrant soul. In J. Hippler and A .Lueg (eds) *The Next Threat.* (eds) London: Pluto Press

Halliday, F (2006) Anti-Arab prejudice in the UK: the Killroy-Silk affair and the BBC Response. In E. Poole and J. Richardson (eds) *Muslims in the News Media.* London: I. B. Tauris

Hardy, J and Vieler-Porter, C (1992) Race, Schooling and the 1988 Education Act in D. Gill, B. Mayor and M. Blair (eds) *Racism and Education Structures and Strategies.* London: Sage Publications

Hastings, A (1987) *A History of English Christianity 1920-1985.* London: Collins

Haywood, M (2008) Shap a brief history. Available http/www.shapworkingparty.org.uk/ history.html

Heater, D (2001) The History of Citizenship Education in England. *Curriculum Journal* 12 (1) p103 – 123

Hobson, J (2004) *The Eastern Origins of Western Civilisation.* Sydney: Sydney University Press

Home Office (2001) *Report of the Independent Review Team: Community Cohesion.* London: TSO

Home Office (2008) *Prevent.* London: TSO

Home Office (2011) *Prevent.* Available at http://www.homeoffice.gov.uk/publications/ counter-terrorism/prevent/prevent-strategy/

HMSO (1981) *The Rampton Report: (West Indian Children in Our Schools)* London: HMSO.

Hull, J (2000) Religionism and Religious Education. In M. Leister, C. Modgil and S Modgil (eds) *Education, Culture and Values: Spiritual and Religious*. London: Falmer Press

Jackson R (1995) Religious Education's Representation of 'Religions' and 'Cultures', *British Journal of Educational Studies*. 43 (3) p272-289

Jackson, R (1999) *Religious Education – an interpretative approach*. London: Hodder and Stoughton

Jackson, R (2004) *Rethinking Religious Education and Plurality*. London: RoutledgeFalmer.

Jackson, R (2004) Intercultural education and recent European pedagogies of religious education. *Intercultural Education*, 15 (1) p4-14

Jackson, R (2011) The interpretative approach as a research tool: inside the REDCo project. *British Journal of Religious Education* 33 (2) p189-208

Jackson, S (2002) *On the Boundaries of Theological Tolerance in Islam*. Oxford: Oxford University Press

Johnston, A (2003) *Missionary Writing and Empire*. Cambridge: Cambridge University Press

Jonker, G and Thobani, S (2010) Interpretations of the Muslim world in European texts. In G. Jonker and S. Thobani (eds) *Narrating Islam*. New York: Tauris Academic Studies

Joppke, C (2004) The Retreat of multiculturalism in the liberal state: theory and policy. *British Journal of Sociology* 55 (2) p237-257

Kay, K (2007) Can Skills Help Religious Education? In (eds) M. Felderhof and D. Torevell *Inspiring Faith in Schools*. Aldershot: Ashgate

Kalin, I (2011) Islamophobia and the limits of multiculturalism. In J. Esposito and I. Kalin (eds) *Islamophobia: the Challenge of Pluralism*. Oxford: Oxford University Press

Khan, K (2009) Preventing Violent Extremism (PVE) and Prevent. Available at http://www. an-nisa.org/...PVE&Prevent.

Khan, M G (2010) No Innocents: Muslims in the Prevent Strategy. In S. Sayyid and A.Vakil (eds) *Thinking Through Islamophobia*. London: Hurst and Company

Khan, S (2002) MuslimWomen: Negotiations in the Third Space. In T. Saliba, A. Allen and J Howard (eds) *Gender, Politics and Islam*. London: University of Chicago Press

Khan, T (2011) RE is more than just about Religion. Available at http://www.luton.gov.uk

Kincheloe, J (1993) The Politics of Race, History and Curriculum. In A. Castenell and W. Pinar (eds) *Understanding Curriculum as Racial Text*. New York: State University of New York Press

Kincheloe, J and Steinberg, S (1997) *Changing Multiculturalism Changing Education*. Buckingham: Open University Press

Kincheloe, J (2010) *Knowledge and Critical Pedagogy*. New York: Springer

Kundnani, A (2007) *The End of Tolerance*. London: Pluto Press

Kundnani, A (2009) *Spooked! How not to prevent violent extremism*. London: Institute of Race Relations

Lees, J (1882) *Mahommedanism in Faiths of the World-St Giles Lectures*. London: William Blackwood and Sons

Lewis, P (1994) *Islamic Britain*. London: I. B. Tauris

Liberty (2010) Liberty's response to the Home Office Consultation on the *Prevent* strand of the UK counter-terrorism strategy. Available at http:// liberty-human-rights.org.uk/publications/1-policy-papers/index.shtml

Little, A and Willey, R (1981) *Multi Ethnic Britain: The Way Forward.* London: Schools Council Project

London Borough of Merton (2008) The Merton Agreed Syllabus for RE. Available at http//:www.merton.gov.uk/_agreed-syllabus_for-religious-education

Loukes, H (1961) *Teenage Religion: an enquiry into attitudes and possibilities among British boys and girls in secondary modern schools.* London: SCM Press

Lundie, D (2010) 'Does RE work?' An analysis of the aims, practices and models of effective RE in the UK. *British Journal of Religious Education.* 32 (2) p163-170

Marshall, H (2010) The Prevent Strategy and Controversies. In J. Schmack, M Thompson, D. Torevell and C. Cole (eds). *Engaging Religion.* Newcastle: Cambridge Scholars Publishing.

Marwick, A (2003) *British Society Since 1945.* London: Penguin

Masuzawa, T (2005) *The Invention of World Religions.* Chicago: University of Chicago Press

Maurice, F (1861) *On the Religions of the World and their relations to Christianity.* London: Macmillan and Co

McClure, K (1990) The Limits of Toleration. *Political Theory* 18 (3) p361-391

McCutcheon, R (2001) *Critics not caretakers: Redescribing the Public Study of Religion.* Albany, NY: State University of New York Press

McGhee, D (2003) 'Moving to 'Our' Common Ground – A Critical Examination of Community Cohesion Discourse in Twenty First Century Britain'. *The Sociological Review.* 51 (3) p376-404

Meer, N (2007) Muslim schools in Britain: challenging mobilisations or logical developments. In *Asian Pacific Education.* 27 (1) p55-71

Miller, J (2010) The contribution of Local Authorities and their SACRES to promoting cohesion through Religious Education. In (ed) M. Grimmitt. *Religious Education and Social and Community Cohesion.* Essex: McCrimmon

Modood, T (1998) Anti-Essentialism, Multiculturalism and the 'Recognition" of Religious Groups. *Journal of Political Philosophy.* 6 (14) p378-399

Modood, T (2010) *Still Not Easy being British.* Stoke on Trent: Trentham

Morey, P and Yaqin, A (2011) *Framing Muslims.* London: Harvard University Press

Murray, A. (1953) *Education into Religion.* London: Nisbet and Co, Ltd

Murti, Kamakshi (2008) To Veil or not to Veil? The *Hijab* as a Marker of Alterity. In S. Martinson and R. Schulz (eds) *Transcultural German Studies.* Oxford: Peter Lang

Ofsted (2007) Making Sense of Religion. Available at http//www.ofsted.gov.uk

Ofsted (2010) Transforming Religious Education. Available at http://www.ofsted.gov.uk

OSCE/ODIHR (2007) Toledo guiding principles on teaching about religions and beliefs in public schools. Available http://www.osce.org/odihr/29154 Assessed May 2011

OSCE/ODIHR (2011) Guidelines for Educators on Countering Intolerance and Discrimination. Available at http://www.osce.org/odihr/84495 Accessed December 2011

Osler, A (2010) Patriotism, citizenship and multiculturalism: Political discourse and the curriculum. In M Grimmitt (ed) *Religious Education and social and Community Cohesion.* Essex: McCrimmmons

Osler, A and Starkey, H (2001) Citizenship Education and national identities in France and England: inclusive or exclusive? *Oxford Review of Education.* 27 (2) p287 – 305

Otterbeck, J (2005) What is Reasonable to Demand? Islam in Swedish Textbooks. *Journal of Ethnic and Migration Studies* 31 (4) p795-812

Owen, S (2011) the World Religions paradigm. *Arts and Humanities in Higher Education* 10 (3) p253-268

Palumbo-Lu, D (2002) Multiculturalism now: civilisation, national identity, and difference before and after September in *Boundary* 2. 29 (2) p109-128

Panjwani, F (2005) Agreed Syllabuses and un-agreed values: Religious Education and Missed Opportunities for Fostering Social Cohesion. *British Journal Educational Studies.* 53 (3) p375-393

Panjwani, F (2010) Religious Education and Islam. Paper presented at a conference 'Islamophobia and Education' British Educational Research Association. March 4 2010. Conference poster available at http//wallscometumblingdown.flies.wordpress.co.m/2010/02/conferences-flyer-2pdf

Panjwani, F (forthcoming) From Islamic Values to 'Religio-secular' Values in Muslim Contexts. In (eds) J. Arthur and T. Lovat, *International Handbook of Religions and Values.* London: Routledge

Parker, S and Freathy, R (2011) Context, complexity and contestation: Birmingham's Agreed Syllabuses for religious education since the 1970s. *Journal of Belief and Values* 32 (2) p247-263

Parsons, C (2008) Race relations legislation, ethnicity and disproportionally in school exclusions in England. *Cambridge Journal of Education.* 38 (3) p401-419

Pearce, S. (2005) *You wouldn't understand – White teachers in multi-ethnic classrooms.* Stoke-on-Trent: Trentham

Phillips, C, Tse, D. Johnson, F (2010) *Community Cohesion and PREVENT: how have schools responded?* London: DoE

Phillips, M (2005) This Lethal Moral Madness. *Daily Mail* 14 July p14-15

Phillips, M (2005) Britain 'Sleepwalking into segregation'. Available http://www.guardian.co.uk/world/sep/19/race.socialexclusion. Accessed May 2011

Phillips, T (2004) Multiculturalism's Legacy is 'Have a Nice Day' Racism. *Guardian*, May 28th

Qualifications and Curriculum Authority (2004) *The Non-Statutory Framework for Religious Education.* London: QCA

Radu, M (2009) *Introducing Islam*, Mason Crest Publishers

Ramadan, T (2010) *The Quest for Meaning.* London: Allen Lane

Rankin, J. (1993) Teaching World Religions in Schools: methods and strategies. In C Erricker, A Brown, M Hayward, D Kadodwala and P Williams (eds). *Teaching World Religions.* Oxford: Heinemann

Razavi, M and Ambuel, D (1997) (eds) *Philosophy, Religion, and the Question of Intolerance.* Albany: State University of New York Press

REC (2009) Everyone matters in the classroom. A practice code for teachers of RE. Available at http://www.recouncil.org.uk/images/stories/pdf/codeofconduct.pdf

Religious Education Council (REC) (2010) Guidance on Community Cohesion. Available at http://www.religiouseducationcouncil.org/content/view/148/78/

Reno, S (1979) Distance in the Study of Religion. *British Journal of Religious Education* 108-110. 1 (3) p108-110

Reuters (2010) Available at http://www.reuters.com/article/2010/0317us-book-campaign-idustre62G41Y20100317

Robinson, D (2008) Community cohesion and the politics of communitarianism in J Flint and D. Robinson (eds). *Community Cohesion in Crisis?* Bristol: Polity Press.

Ruf, H (1997) Radicalising Liberalism and Modernity. In M. Razavi and D. Ambuel (eds) *Philosophy, Religion and the Question of Intolerance.* Albany: State University of New York Press

Runnymede Trust (1997) Islamophobia: A Challenge for us all. Available at www.runnymedetrust.org/publications/17/32.html

Sahin, A (2010) The Contribution of Religious Education to Social and Community Cohesion: An Islamic educational perspective in M Grimmitt (ed), *Religious Education and Social and Community Cohesion.* Essex: McCrimmons

Saliba, T (2002) *Gender, Politics and Islam.* London: University of Chicago Press

Said, E (1991) *Orientalism.* London: Penguin

Schools Council (1971) *Religious Education in Secondary Schools, Schools Council Working Paper* 36. London: Evans

Schools Council (1977) *Journeys into Religion.* London: Harper Collins

Schools Council Religious Education (1977) *Journey into Religion Teachers handbook.* St Albans: Granada Publishing Limited

Schweitzer, Friedrich (2009) Religious individualization: new challenges to education for tolerance. *British Journal of Education.* 29 (1) p 89 – 100

Sewell, G (2008) *Islam in the Classroom: what the textbooks tell us.* New York: American Textbook Council

Shaheen, J (2008) *Guilty: Hollywood's Verdict on Arabs after 9/11.* New York: Olive Branch

Sheridan, L and Gillett, P (2005) Major World Events and Discrimination in *Asian Journal of Social Psychology,* 8 p191-197

Smalley, S (2005) Teaching about Islam and learning about Muslims: Islamophobia in the classroom. *Resource* 27 (2) p4 – 7

Smart, N. (1968) *Secular Education and the Logic of Religion.* London: Faber and Faber

Smith, W (1978) *The Meaning and End of Religion.* New York: Harper and Row Publishers

Stanley, B (1990) *The Bible and the Flag.* Illinois: Intervarsity Press

Teece, G (2011) Too Many Competing Imperatives? Does RE need to rediscover its identity? *Journal of Belief and Values.* Vol 32. No. 2 p161-172

Thobani, S (2010) *Islam in the School Curriculum.* London: Continuum

Tinker, C (2009) Rights, social cohesion and identity: arguments for and against state funded Muslim schools in Britain. *Race, Ethnicity and Education.* 12 (4) p539-553

Thompson, M (2010) Reflecting honestly: Ideological conflict, Religious Education and community cohesion. In M. Grimmitt (ed) *Religious Education and Social and Community Cohesion*. Essex: McCrimmons

Tomlinson, S (1983). The Educational needs of ethnic minority children. *Journal of Biosocial Science*, 15, p157-166

Tomlinson, S (1996) Teacher Education for a Multicultural Britain. In M Craft (ed) *Teacher Education in Plural Societies – An International Review*. London: Falmer Press

Tomlinson, S (2008) *Race and Education*. Maidenhead: Open University Press

Townsend, H and Brittan, E (1972) *Organisation in Multiracial Schools*. Windsor: NFER – Nelson

Travis, A (2011) Axe funding for anti-democracy Muslim groups says former minister. Available at http://www.guardian.co.uk/politics/2011/jun/07/muslim-groups-counter-terrorism-funding

Troyna, B. (1983) Multiracial education: just another brick in the wall? *New Community*, 10. p424 – 428.

Tyler, A (2008) *Islam, the West and Tolerance*. Basingstoke: Palgrave Macmillan

Vakil A K (2010) Is the Islam in Islamophobia the same as the Islam in Anti-Islam; or, When is it Islamophobia Time? In S Sayyid and A. K. Valik (eds) *Thinking Through Islamophobia: Global Perspectives*. London: Hurst and Company p23-43.

Wakefield Agreed Syllabus (2007) Available at http//:www.wakefield.gov.uk/.../04_Agreed_Syllabus

Weisse, W (2011) The European research-project on Religion and Education 'REDCo' an introduction. In R, Jackson, S. Miedema, W. Weisse and J-P. Willaime (eds) *Religion and Education in Europe*. Munster: Waxmann

Werbner, P (2005) The Translocation of culture: 'community cohesion' and the force of multiculturalism in history. *The Sociological Review* 53 (4) p 745-768

Winch, C (2005) Developing a critical rationality as a pedagogical aim in F. Heyting and C. Winch (eds) *Conformism and Critique in Liberal Society*. Oxford: Blackwell Publishing

Worcestershire County Council (2009) Agreed Syllabus. Available at https: //www.Edulink.networcs.net. Accessed July 2011

Worley, C (2005) 'It's not about race. It's about community.': New Labour and 'community cohesion'. *Critical Social Policy* 25 (4) p483-496

Wright, A (2004) *Religion, Education and Post-modernity*. London: RoutledgeFalmer

Wright, A. (2007) *Critical religious education, multiculturalism and the pursuit of truth*. Cardiff: University of Wales Press

Wright, A and Brandom, A (2000) *Learning to Teach Religious Education in the Secondary School*. London: RoutledgeFalmer

Zagorin, P (2003) *How the Idea of Religious Tolerance Came to the West*. Princeton: Princeton University Press

Zebiri, K (2011) Orientalist Themes in Contemporary Islamophobia. In J. Esposito and I. Kalin (eds) *The Challenge of Pluralism in the 21st Century*. Oxford: Oxford University Press

Index

agreed syllabus 6, 7, 26, 27, 74, 75, 102, 104
An-Nisa Society 80
arranged marriage 52, 54, 61
Asian 22, 24, 31, 57
assimilation 22, 23, 34- 36, 50, 69, 78, 104

Birmingham Agreed Syllabus 5
Britishness 32, 35, 36, 78, 111, 105, 106, 117

Cameron, D 21, 36, 73
Cantle Report 68
Christianity
    and confessionalism/ Christian education 3, 4-5, 15-16, 27
    and empire 8-9
citizenship education 40, 46, 52, 53, 58, 77
colonialism 91
Commission for Racial Equality 21, 27
community cohesion 66-78
    and Islam/Muslims 68, 70, 73
    and the Religious Education Council (REC) 77
    criticism of 75-76

policy 41, 60, 66
    the role of schools 67-68
comparative religion 14, 16
Contest 36, 78-80, 108, 111
Copley, T 8, 13, 14, 16, 55, 104
critical approaches to education 98, 115-118

Department for Children, Schools and families (DCSF) 40, 41, 42, 49, 88

Education Reform Act 5, 25
equality 63, 80
ethnicity 36, 50, 56, 114
extremism 60, 66, 84-85, 92

faith schools 71
Five Pillars of Islam 2, 111

Grimmitt, M 74-75, 77

Hajj 2
hijab 60, 62
history textbooks 37
Home Office 26, 65, 67, 70, 77, 79, 86, 109, 117

immigrants 22, 23, 50, 56, 57 *see also* immigration
integration 22, 23, 34-36, 50, 69, 72, 78, 105-106, 107, 117 *see also* assimilation
Islam
    and curriculum 5, 116-117
    and extremism/ fundamentalism 36, 60, 107, 109, 110
    and international conflict 32, 56, 105
    and multiculturalism 22, 26, 32-34, 106
    and religious education 13, 36
    as a world religion 6, 12-13, 16
    relationship to Christianity 5, 8, 9-10, 11, 14, 19, 56
Islamophobia 33, 46, 47, 54, 58, 63, 93, 98, 116, 117

Jackson, R 9, 28, 108, 109, 115
jihad 37
Joseph Rowntree Charitable Trust 80

liberal values 15, 21, 34,
55-56, 64, 73, 106
Liberty 80

Mohammedism 3, 9, 11, 14
Miller, J 65
misrepresentation 44, 46,
53, 54, 59, 112, 113,
114
multiculturalism
and Islam 22, 32-34
and religious education
22, 28,
and tolerance 103, 106
criticism of 21-22, 29,
32, 36, 106, 113
origins 23
Muslim(s)
and integration 21
communities 31, 33, 65,
70, 107, 112, 117
criminalisation of 80-81,
83
identity 22, 24, 31, 32
publishing houses 46,
48, 49
schools 71
women 33, 38, 50, 60-
64, 103, 107-108

National Curriculum 29, 30-
31
niqab 33, 36, 50, 51, 60
French ban 61, 62
Non-Statutory Framework
for Religious Education
88, 100

objectivity 16, 92
Ofsted 30, 39, 63
omission 53, 93-96
orientalism 40, 46, 47, 59,
62, 64, 97, 118

Other 7, 62, 64, 98, 101,
114, 116

Panjwani, F 43, 44, 45, 55,
59, 108, 110
Prevent 36, 65, 73-86, 104,
105, 110, 111, 117
criticisms of 80-81, 86
race
and education 24, 28,
116
and integration 35
racial inequality 22, 23, 25,
85
radicalism 21, 39
REDCo 114
religious education
and Islam 5, 13, 18, 73,
108, 111, 113
and multiculturalism 26-
29, 103
and REsilience 88, 105
and tolerance 100, 111,
103, 105
and values 29
and world religions 6,
12-18
approach to neutrality
92, 99, 104
debates and
pedagogies 3, 93, 99,
108, 109, 111-112, 113,
114, 115
history of 3, 6, 13
research into 40-3
schools council 16, 17,
18
social and community
cohesion 73-78, 110
Religious Education
Council (REC) 74, 77,
83
Code of Practice 99, 100
and REsilience 87

Religious Studies 17
representation 112, 114,
117
by omission 59, 71, 75,
89-90, 93-96, 107
disinterested 116
neutral 38, 52, 92, 104,
105
of Muslim women 50,
60, 61, 90, 107
REsilience
and religious education
87, 93-94, 109
and role of the teacher
87, 89
and schools 86-96, 109
Gateways 88-94
preventing the spread
of extremism 87, 66
riots 23, 24, 69, 88
Runnymede Trust 54
Rushdie, S 31, 32

secularism 15, 33, 34
Shap 13, 16, 17, 27
Stephen Lawrence Inquiry
37

teachers
neutral teaching 88, 99
role of the teacher 39,
41, 53, 82, 84, 88,
89,95, 109, 117
teacher training 25, 28
terrorism 39, 56, 60, 79,
81, 84
textbooks
and exams 40, 42, 49
inaccuracies 42, 43
misrepresentation of
Islam 44
Toledo Guiding Principles
100, 116

toleration/tolerance
  and diversity 101, 102
  and Islam 101, 109,
  110-111
  and multiculturalism
  103, 106
  and the Other 98
  and religious education
  100, 103
  promotion of 98
Twin Towers/9/11 32, 62,
  78, 107, 109

values
  British 36, 97-98, 117
  importance of 70, 73,
  76, 86, 101, 110, 113
  Muslim 31, 34, 35, 36,
  69, 97
  shared 66, 72, 77, 79,
  82
veil 50, 51, 62-63, 103 *see
also* hijab; niqab
Victorians 10, 12

Westhill Project 49
World religions
  and Christianity 14, 16,
  and empire 8, 9, 11
  and Religious
  Education 12
  origins 6-7, 10
  place of Islam 7, 12, 16